LEARNING TO TEACH

By Richard B. Dierenfield

CENTURY TWENTY ONE PUBLISHING

PUBLISHED BY

CENTURY TWENTY ONE PUBLISHING
POST OFFICE BOX 8
SARATOGA, CALIFORNIA 95070

LIBRARY OF CONGRESS CARD CATALOG NUMBER

80-69119

I.S.B.N.

0-86548-031-1

TABLE OF CONTENTS

DEDICATION.. V

PREFACE..VII

CHAPTER I. LEARNING TO TEACH.. 1
 The Learning Pattern... 2
 Feedback Sources for the Teacher..................................... 3
 The Three-legged Stool Analogy....................................... 4

CHAPTER II. WHAT ARE YOU TRYING TO TEACH? THE IMPORTANCE OF AIMS........ 7

CHAPTER III. PLANNING PAYS OFF.. 14
 Long Range Plans... 16
 Intermediate Range Plans... 19
 Short Range Plans.. 25
 Daily Lesson Plan Form... 27

CHAPTER IV. ORGANIZE YOUR INSTRUCTION FOR BEST RESULTS................... 30
 Teaching Understandings.. 31
 Teaching Skills.. 34
 Teaching Attitudes... 36

CHAPTER V. INSTRUCTIONAL SKILLS YOU WILL NEED........................... 41
 Achieving Instructional Set.. 42
 Obtaining Closure.. 44
 Reinforcement.. 45
 Feedback... 48
 Focusing... 50
 Style Variation.. 50

CHAPTER VI. HOW TO HANDLE BASIC TEACHING METHODS........................ 54
 The Lecture.. 55
 The Discussion... 61

CHAPTER VII. HOW TO ACHIEVE CLARITY IN TEACHING......................... 71

CHAPTER VIII. NO CONTROL?.....NO LEARNING!.............................. 82
 Preventive Discipline.. 89
 Corrective Discipline.. 95

CHAPTER IX. HAVE YOUR STUDENTS LEARNED ANYTHING?......................100
    A Few Important Concepts................................100
    Organize Your Efforts..................................105
    Some Principles of Making Up Examinations..............106
    Constructing Test Items................................111
    True-False Questions...................................112
    Multiple Choice Questions..............................114
    Matching Questions.....................................115
    Completion (or fill in) Questions......................116
    Essay Questions..118
    Marking Subjective Items...............................121

CHAPTER X. THE TEN COMMANDMENTS OF TEACHING...................123

ACKNOWLEDGEMENTS

To

"Bruce and David"

PREFACE

"Learning To Teach" may seem to be a very ambitious title for such a small book. This apparent paradox does not arise because I take the subject lightly. On the contrary it is so crucial that a short, concise treatment is essential. The topics covered here relate directly to the problems faced by every person who attempts to teach others. The beginning teacher asks the questions, "What Can I Do?" and "How Can I Go About Doing It?" They require immediate and practical aid. There is no shortage of books with a heavy theoretical and philosophical base. I do not mean to disparage such treatments of the subject but there is a real need for a straight-forward, uncomplicated exposition of teaching.

Following a long but unsuccessful search, for such a basic volume I decided to write one myself. After many years of teaching and working in teacher education a number of things have become clear to me about instructing others and learning how to do it well. I have tried to concentrate and distill a number of these ideas into the pages of this book. Hopefully you will find it useful in learning how to teach. The market for good teachers never exceeds the supply. May this book help you start on the right foot!

Richard B. Dierenfield

St. Paul, Minnesota

CHAPTER 1

LEARNING TO TEACH

Teaching is one of the most common of human activities. It takes the place not only in schools but in the arenas of business and commerce, in the relationship between doctor and patient, lawyer and client and salesperson and customer or wherever ideas are exchanged and new behavior desired. Since teaching is so widespread and important the need for effective instructional practice is clear.

This little book is directed toward anyone who intends to teach, whether it be one person tutoring another or someone involved with large groups. There are a number of basic principles and ideas which, when mastered as teaching skills will go a long way to produce that rare individual, a truly effective teacher. We will direct our attention to these fundamental concepts in the following pages.

Teaching is a very complex activity which has been studied, analyzed and researched for many years. The result has been a mass of literature, much of it quite esoteric and specialized, which does little to help those who are just learning how to do it. This volume aims at assisting the beginner and as more of a "first aid mannual" than an advanced treatise on brain surgery. It is written in direct, straightforward language with much unnecessary professional jargon eliminated. The documentation and supplementary reading lists common in textbooks will not be found. Our objective is simply to help you become familiar with sound teaching techniques. In order to become an effective instructor, however, you will need to have more than the knowledge of how to teach.

The Learning Pattern

This knowledge must be translated into techniques and these must be applied with skill and insight in a live situation with real learners. Such a process often follows this pattern of development:

1) The "learning teacher" becomes conscious of the need to understand the teaching act.

2) He/she learns the principles of teaching.

3) These concepts are practiced in a real situation.

4) Skill is gained in applying sound teaching approaches through continued use.

5) Crucial to such practice is the feedback you receive from the learners. Do they respond to and learn from your teaching methods?

6) Finally, this learner response is evaluated and whatever modification is indicated must take place.

Then, the process begins again reverting back to the principles, knowing them, applying them, practicing them over and over, receiving feedback and once more evaluating and modifying.

The old axiom holds true: "unless learning is taking place, no teaching is being accomplished."

Feedback Sources for the Teacher

Since evaluation of instructional skills is so important to you in learning how to teach we will take note of some useful sources of this reaction.

Yourself. "Would some power the giftie give us to see ourselves as others see us." Most teacher improvement comes as a result of the individual efforts put forth by each person desiring to grow. In this process it is necessary to set personal goals and to examine what is being done by yourself in an objective manner. If this type of analysis is consistently sought and realistically used your performance is very likely to improve.

Other teachers. Invite other teachers especially experienced ones to visit your classes and provide analysis of your teaching patterns and practices. If you are having particular problems ask the observer to concentrate on the difficult area. Advice-giving is generally a pleasurable activity and most seasoned practitioners are glad to share their experience with you.

Learners. You will, almost inevitably receive reaction from those you teach. There are several kinds of such feedback and if you "read" them cor- rectly you will be able to learn much about the strengths and weaknesses of your teaching style.

A. Non-verbal. Often no word need be spoken since the looks and actions of your learners will tell you a great deal of what they are comprehending and

3

how they are feeling about you and your instructional approaches.

B. Informal verbal. This involves spoken questions and answers in recitation or discussion or even learner talk not directly related to the subject under consideration.

C. Informal written. Evidence of your teaching abilities can be gleaned from tests, worksheets, papers or any written work in which learners show or apply ideas you have tried to teach them.

D. Formal written. This is a direct approach to students feelings about a teacher's instructional ability through a checklist of skills and qualities to be completed by the learners themselves.

Mechanical devices. The video and audio tape machines do help us "see ourselves as others see us." The T.V. tape of your teaching techniques although traumatic to some will give you a real "learner's eye" view of how you look and sound to your class. The adio tape, while it provides only a one dimensional feedback, can teach much. It is important to view (or listen) these tapes with particular points in mind. A list of what you seek to learn from these feedback devices will help you rise above the superficial level such as counting the number of times you say "okay." Much of fundamental worth can be recovered, e.g., the type and thoughtfulness of your questions, the clarity of your explanations, the organization and integration of your ideas, etc.

The Three-Legged Stool Analogy

Teaching can be compared to a three-legged stool which requires all its legs to function as it should.

One leg is knowledge of subject matter. Depth and breadth in your teaching

Knowledge of Subject   Teaching Technique

Personality

area will enable you to know what is important, how ideas are related and

help you decide on the best sequence of presentation. An old saying has it

that, "You can teach what you don't know just as well as you can come back

from where you have never been."

Another leg is personality. Although there is no "ideal" or "typical"

teacher type you must be able to deal successfully with the age and kind of

learner in your class. Surveys of learners consistently reveal they value

such personality qualities as "pleasantness," "firmness," "patience," "sense

of humor," and "concern for individual feelings." The good teacher will re-

late professionally with learners but may not be personally popular with all

of them. A sense of balance in human relationships is of great worth in

teaching experience.

The last leg is teaching techniques. That is what this book is all about.

Hopefully, if you have a sound grasp of your subject matter and a pleasant

personality the help with instructional approaches supplied in this volume

will aid you in becoming a successful teacher.

The act of teaching is a highly personal and individual affair. Each

person brings to the instructional process such qualities, experiences, back-

ground, level of subject knowledge and teaching techniques as to result in a totally unique entity. The principles, concepts and skills suggested in these pages will be applied in somewhat different ways by each of you. They will be integrated with the other parts of your total being and finally become your "teaching style." Although the basics of instruction remain the same their application into your personal teaching patterns will remain a matter of individual feeling and ability. The resulting satisfaction from developing into a competent teacher with your own "professional touch" will be worth all the effort that will be required.

CHAPTER 2

WHAT ARE YOU TRYING TO TEACH? - THE IMPORTANCE OF AIMS

This is the fundamental question which a teacher must constantly ask. Aims are the benchmark from which everything in teaching begins and are therefore of crucial significance.

Aims do not appear to you by magic out of the blue. You must think of them and often they require a considerable amount of mental effort. They are the values which provide thrust and direction for teaching at any level. Everything: content, teaching-learning activities, materials, etc. should grow out of your objectives not visa versa.

Simply stated, objectives are those things you want your learners to know, be able to do or to feel after you have finished the instruction. It is not to be expected that each student will reach every goal. Many objectives will be mastered and those that are not will provide a guide toward which to work.

In this chapter we will look at the various types of goals and offer suggestions on how to set up both long range and immediate objectives. At this point I want to establish the main categories of aims which we can use in our consideration of the subject. Often in reading about modern goal setting the literature refers to a three fold classification of educational objectives. This grouping was first brought out by a man named Benjamin Bloom in 1956. The three divisions were as follows:

1) The Cognitive Domain - refers to the acquisition and manipulation of factual information.

2) The Affective Domain - involves itself with feelings, values and emotions.

3) The Psychomotor Domain - concerns the development of physiological skills.

After having done this I want to suggest another somewhat similar system of classifying teaching aims. It is simpler and easier to understand. There are also three areas involved as follows:

1) Understanding. When a learner has achieved a true understanding he/she not only knows the facts and data involved but can apply and evaluate the ideas involved.

Examples:

A) The learner will understand the causes of the Great Depression of 1929.

B) The learner will understand the Law of Supply and Demand.

2) Attitudes. Here again when the learner has developed attitudes he/she will have taken on certain specified emotional approaches, values and feelings as a result of the instructional experiences which have taken place.

<u>Examples</u>:

A) The learner will approach new ideas with objectivity and will suspend judgment until evidence has been examined.

B) The learner will operate machinery with enough caution and care to insure safety.

3) <u>Skills</u>. The acquisition of this type of learning objective deals with developing <u>specified habitual responses</u> of <u>both</u> a <u>physical</u> and <u>mental</u> <u>nature</u>.

<u>Examples</u>:

A) The learner will be skilled in using library resources to locate desired information.

B) The learner will be skilled in the operation of a metal lathe.

These categories are not discrete or permanently separated. They often overlap beginning in one area and leading into another. Attitudes frequently begin with certain understandings. We have all had the experience of being required to learn something which has led us into a great liking for or interest in a particular activity. Another illustration of this point can be seen in skills which nearly always originate as knowledges of processes. These patterns are repeated and practiced until they become nearly habitual and automatic.

Let us now turn from classifying aims to examine goals in terms of their coverage: long range or broad in scope and immediate or specific and narrowly defined.

Broad, long range objectives provide general guidelines for handling instruction over larger time periods from two weeks and more. The broadness of the objectives is usually in direct proportion to the length of time involved.

While these general objectives have real value in defining the scope and coverage of learning they do present some difficulties. The most pressing and serious problem is that since they are so general they cannot be used to provide guides for immediate, short range instructional efforts. They are often framed in such vague, nebulous language that some teachers have hidden behind them with little or no intention of actually using them. For this reason a movement has spread in recent years to break general objectives up into smaller component parts. These more specific aims are called "implementing objectives" since they help teachers apply larger goals to more pointed less extensive learning situations. Because they have been commonly stated in terms of desired behaviors which result from instruction they are called "behavioral objectives". They are worded in specific terms and focus on the particular actions which will demonstrate the desired achievement. The verbs used are active and not the passive type sometimes found in general objectives. A broad goal which is thus divided into several component aims not only helps "point" instruction it assists in the measurement of achievement as well.

The following examples are offered to help clarify the concept of behavioral objectives:

Sample behavioral objectives in the area of skills.

1)   The learner will be able to saw a straight cut of at least two feet in a piece of one inch stock fir wood.

2)   The learner will be able to write a paragraph of at least four sentences in which verbs and subjects agree in number.

3)   The learner will be able to operate a microscope using both large and fine focusing mechanisms.

Sample behavioral objectives in the area of understanding.

1)   The learner will be able to identify the three primary causes for the Depression of 1929.

2)   The learner will be able to clearly explain the parts and function of an automobile braking system.

3)   The learner will be able to list the most important characteristic of Baroque music.

Sample behavioral objectives in the area of attitudes

1)   The learner will show an interest in current events by reading the news section of a newspaper or news magazine when not required to do so.

2)   The learner will demonstrate open mindedness by listening to an opposing point of view without interrupting the speaker.

3)   The learner will indicate pride of workmanship by refinishing part of a woodshop project when not required to do so for a good mark.

As you can see it takes some thought and practice to be able to write effective behavioral (implementing) objectives. However the effort will be well repaid in terms of more effective teaching.

One more point needs to be made in connection with our discussion of objectives. It is essential that you list of hoped for learner achievements be realistic. Many beginning teachers have been frustrated by expecting too much from those being taught. When setting your aims for instruction remember the following factors:

1) Age of the learners

2) Previous educational experience of learners

3) How alike or different members of the learning group are in terms of ability, interest, maturity and background.

4) Your own skill and knowledge as a teacher.

5) The instructional materials and facilities you will have available.

6) The length and frequency of time periods open for learning.

I simply cannot let the subject of goal setting pass without mentioning a word of caution. This involves expecting too little from your learners. It is called the "Pygmalion Effect" or the "Self Fulfilling Prophecy." When you as a teacher, directly or indirectly, indicate that you feel learners cannot or will not be able to achieve a goal the learners tend to doubt their own ability and stop attempting to achieve the task. Often, though not always to be sure, if you expect learners to stretch to master certain skills, ideas and attitudes they will rise to the occasion and happily surprise you and themselves as well.

In our discussion of objectives a number of ideas have been stressed.

Aims are important as they set the dimensions and provide the thrust for teaching.

Aims have been divided into three general, though often overlapping, categories, skills, understandings and attitudes.

Two kinds of aims are commonly used by teachers: general, stated in broad terms and behavioral, stated in specific terms.

Aims, to be worthwhile, must be realistic, taking into consideration the conditions of teaching and the characteristics of the learners.

The measure of whether you have chosen ahievable aims and taught effectively is likely to come in your assessment activities. When you evaluate make sure you are seeking evidence that your learners have mastered the goals of instruction set up at the beginning of the teaching period.

Take some time as you begin each instructional module, be it a year, a month or a day, to set out in simple terms the learning objectives to be achieved. The effort will be repaid many fold by the increase in your teaching efficiency.

CHAPTER 3

PLANNING PAYS OFF

All good teachers plan. It is an important key to successful teaching.

Beginning teachers find detailed plans an indispensible source of aid and

while experienced personnel do not require the same specifics, planning is

still a must. Trying to achieve the aims of a lesson or a course without

making instructional plans is as difficult as building a house without blueprints.

Planning serves several vital functions in your teaching.

1) It provides the organization and direction for clear, understandable

instruction.

2) It helps you to avoid forgetting important ideas.

3) It assists you to guard against improper emphasis.

4) It enables you to place ideas in a logical and understandable se-

quence of presentation.

5) It gives you a feeling of confidence and assurance as you teach.

6) It allows you to take time to select the most effective activities for the achievement of instructional aims.

7) It aids you in choosing the best available learning materials ahead of the time for instruction.

8) It permits you to decide the amount of time to be spent on the topics to be studied.

Are you convinced? I hope so as it is such a foundation stone of good teaching. We will now examine the anatomy of instructional planning and offer you some help in making your own plans.

Planning can be divided into three general levels depending on the length of time involved.

1) Long range plans - deals broadly with the total subject matter of a whole course or even a sequence of several courses, i.e., all the English composition grammar and literature in schools from kindergarten through 12th grade.

2) Intermediate range plans - involves preparing for each of the major themes and subdivisions of a course.

3) Short range plans - concentrates usually on single lessons sometimes weekly plans for one class.

Each plan should be related to the next longer range plan of which it is a part so that the whole hangs together well. If follows, therefore, that you should proceed from long range to intermediate to short range plans. The following diagram will help to show this interrelationship.

We will now deal with the mechanics of planning for the various time

	UNIT I (2 weeks)	UNIT II (3 weeks)	UNIT III (3 weeks)	UNIT IV (3 weeks)

Whole
Course-
(Long
Range)
30 weeks
150 days

Units-
(Intermediate)
(Range)

Days-
(Short
Range)

UNIT V			
		UNIT VI (3 weeks)	UNIT VII (3 weeks)

UNIT VIII

Day (5 weeks)

1	2	3	4	5
6	7	8	9	10
11	12	13	14	15
16	17	18	19	20
21	22	23	24	25

UNIT IX (4 weeks)   UNIT X (4 weeks)

categories shown in the preceding diagram. What you actually will put into the plans will be a combination of your own ideas and the matters covered in Chapters IV, V and VI.

Long Range Plans

These plans will be rather general, covering broad areas of content and large instructional approaches. In making your long range plans you must consider each of the following matters and make decisions on how to deal with the problems involved in each.

1) Aims of the course. This covers the essential question, "What are the learners to learn?" divided into skills, understandings and attitudes.

2) Main topics and concepts. What important ideas, principles, skills, knowledges, etc. are involved in the course?

3) <u>Organization of the course</u>. How do you plan to structure the ideas of your courses? You must decide how to divide the central ideas of the course in such a way as to make them most interesting and understandable. Some examples of course organization are:

By Topics
Chronologically
Simple to Complex
Concrete to Abstract
Practical to Theoretical
Others

4) <u>Sequencing the material</u>. The need for a meaningful order of presentation of ideas in teaching is evident. In some subjects, i.e., mathematics, a step by step approach is required since later topics depend on understanding knowledge gained earlier. In other areas simple logic indicates that a particular sequence is best for creating interest or increasing clarity.

5) <u>General time schedule</u>. This will be decided upon as you look over the main topics to be incorporated in the course and make decisions on how much emphasis each will receive. Will power must be used to stick to this timetable. In doing this you will avoid the hazard which is typical of many beginning American history teachers. So much time may be spent on relatively unimportant matters such as the War of 1812 that no time is left at the end of the course to consider anything after World War II.

6) <u>Learning materials</u>. It is essential that you accumulate, or know where you can obtain material which will help learners master the ideas of the course.

This includes such items as:

<u>Reading materials</u>

Textbooks - appropriate to the common reading level but also include some resources for those <u>above</u> and <u>below</u> the average reading level.

Additional sources - standard references collateral reading pamphlets, periodicals, etc.

Specialized hardware - in particular areas such as music, art, science, wood and metal shop, physical education equipment needed must be noted and obtained.

Community resources - should include both places you can take your learners <u>and</u> outside resource people who can go to your classroom.

Audio-visual aids - locate <u>and be able to use</u> the multitude of helpful devices such as: blackboards, pictures, maps, charts, tapes, records, sound films, film strips, slides, overhead and opaque projectors.

7) <u>Teaching methods</u>. Write down ideas on activities you will engage in to help learners achieve the aims of the course. These should be noted near the ideas, concepts, skills, attitudes for which they apply on your plan sheets.

8) <u>Learning methods</u>. These will include what you will provide for your

class to do in mastering the material to be studied. <u>It is crucial</u> to remember to gear the teaching-learning methods to: the aims of the course, the maturity of the class and the ability(ies) of the learners. Also keep in mind that <u>variety</u> is necessary in both teaching and learning methods to avoid boring your students and to capitalize on the variety of learning styles represented in your class.

9) <u>Evaluation devices</u>. When planning how to teach a particular subject it is very helpful to include a program to measure progress toward the achievement of course goals. These measurement instruments should be noted in your general plans as you write them out. Such items should be included as: written exercises, translations, worksheets, short quizzes, oral and written reports, major exams, projects of all kinds, etc.

All of the above rather extensive list of course planning suggestions may be somewhat confusing to you. It is possible to use these ideas in a structured planning form and help to simplify what may appear complicated. The course plan sheet on the following page can serve to organize your approach to the problem of laying out the materials and methods of study. As a suggestion - a weeks worth of work can be put down on one of these forms. The 8½" x 14", "legal size" sheet is well suited for this purpose.

Intermediate Range Plans

After you have completed your long range plans for the entire course it is wise to give attention to the major topics you intend to include. When the course is considered as a very large aspect of human knowledge it is possible to subdivide it into its most important component part. These sections will

COURSE PLANNING FORM
(8½" x 14")

Subject of Course: _____

Unit Topic: _____

AIMS	TOPIC AND CONCEPTS	LEARNING ACT.	TEACHING ACT.	TIME SCHEDULE	INSTRUCTIONAL MATERIALS	EVALUATION PROCESSES
What will be learned	Subject matter outline or list	What learners will do	What teacher will do	How much time will be spent	Printed material, films-records maps, etc.	Tests, papers, quizzes, etc.

20

now be examined.

They are called "units" because they are central themes or major ideas in a course. The material and teaching strategies are organized around these dominant subtopics because learners can more clearly comprehend ideas if they are related to a known theme or concept. This unity provides a valuable cohesion and relationship among all the ideas involved thus increasing the likelihood of understanding and retention.

How large the topic will be and how extensively it will be considered depend on the academic level of the class. A theme which may be a unit on one level (high school physics unit on "magnetism," for example) might be a whole course in a college setting.

Among many possible illustrations of unit topics are the following: (on the high school level)

Science - Electricity (Physics)
American History - Westward Expansion
English - Poetry
Music - Folk Song
Mathematics - Similarity

You can see that large, course-length subjects, can be subdivided into understandable and manageable parts which can be taught with greater clarity.

Now that you have these unit themes in mind we will deal with planning to teach them. In a way instructing a unit is similar to handling a small course. Each unit is related to the predominant theme of the course and has common threads tying it with other topics.

Unit plans need to be written out and a convenient starting point can be what you have already put down in your long range course plans. They should however, be more detailed and will focused on the group of learners you will be teaching. In preparing a unit plan several important sections must be included which will frame up what and how you will deal with the instruction of the subject matter. Each working unit plan should consider the following matters.

I. <u>Title or name of the unit</u>. It should be crystal clear to the learners <u>what</u> they will be studying.

II. <u>Aims</u>. The skills, understandings and attitudes to be developed through study of the unit must be pinpointed so that learners will realize <u>why</u> the unit is being studied.

III. <u>Pre-assessment</u>. Included here are the processes used by the teacher to determine the nature and extent of prior learner knowledge and attitude about the unit topic. Methods often used to discover the information are short pre-tests (non-graded simple diagnostic examinations) or discussions.

IV. <u>List of terms</u>. In order to understand most new subject areas the learners will need to know the meaning of the words particular to the topic involved. Making a list of such words in preparation for teaching them will help sensitize you to the matter of needed vocabulary mastery.

V. <u>Subject matter outline</u>. This is an organization of the ideas, know-ledges, etc. covering the material necessary to achieve the aims of the unit. It is convenient to put this into a topical outline with major and subpoints as required to include essential content.

VI. <u>Teaching-learning activities</u>. These activities are coupled because of their close, often complementary relationship. In completing this section you should put down, in separate lists what you will do and what the learners will be asked to do. Since the instruction of units can easily be handled in three stages it will be helpful to you if these activities are listed in these three steps: initiatory, developmental and culminating.

A. Initiatory. (Beginning or Starting the Unit)

In this stage of instruction a teacher does several things. You should compile ideas directed to handle these functions:

1) Overview the unit topic for the class.

2) Relate it to previously learned material and general subject theme.

3) Indicate why the topic is important and point out the aims to be achieved.

4) Acquaint the class with the methods of teaching and learning to be followed.

5) Note the means of evaluation to be used.

It is very important to get the study of a unit off to a good start since if the learners are not clear on the "what, how and why" of the enterprise much of what follows may be a waste of time.

B. Developmental. (Continuing and Expanding the Unit)

This second step in teaching the unit is directed at achieving the aims which have been set forth. The instructional activities in this stage will include many more teaching-learning processes than the other two. You must coordinate the aims of the unit with the activities in this section as what goes on in this stage of unit teaching will very likely determine the effectiveness of the whole effort.

C. Culminating. (Closing or Terminating the Unit)

This last of the three steps is designed to bring the unit to a successful close. It will help you to note down ideas on handling the following culminating processes:

1) Review and emphasize the main ideas of the unit.

2) Point out the application of what has been learned.

3) Indicate the progress made by the learners and help them to a feeling of accomplishment.

4) Tie loose ends together and clear up misconceptions which may have arisen in the learner's mind.

5) Connect what has been learned in this unit to the substance of the up-coming unit. This articulation or building bridges between ideas is one of the real signs of an effective teacher.

This culminating section will not take a great amount of time. If the whole unit lasts for fifteen hours of instructional time the initiatory and culminating parts might each take from one to three hours, depending on the circumstances of the class.

VII. Evaluation. This section contains activities which will provide knowledge to both you and your students on progress toward achievement of unit goals. Remember that this process should take place, not only at the end of instruction but as the class moves through the unit. The variety of these activities is virtually endless involving oral and written examinations, exercises, projects, demonstration of skills, etc. If you have framed you objectives in behavioral terms this evaluation aspect will be made easier since the behavior indicated will often suggest the means of measurement.

VIII. <u>Learning Material</u>. This final part of your unit plan will include teaching-learning resources you will use. <u>Appropriate and available</u> instructional materials must be located through investigation of your own collection, plus what you can find in the school and community. Fundamental printed material such as textbooks, periodicals, pamphlets, etc. must be readable by the learners and should include sources for poor readers as well as those who are average or advanced. In addition you will need to search out such audio-visual items as films, tapes, records, film strips, slides, maps, charts, etc. Your plans also may be influenced by whether or not such equipment as television receivers, video tape machines, scientific equipment and other apparatus are available for your use in teaching.

Short Range Plans

Since we are proceeding from the general to the particular in planning we will now consider how to deal with small periods of time, specifically the daily lesson plan. This is the tactical, immediate, action blueprint of what you will do in a single class on a given day. It is most often made sometime between meetings of the same class as it must be tailor made for each class period. To be of maximum usefulness your plans should:

1) Be <u>written out</u>.

2) Be brief and not too elaborated.

3) <u>Not</u> include lecture notes, discussion questions, etc. (These should be separate so as not to make a bulky and confusing lesson plan.)

The actual form of the plan is not important so long as you can work with it and it includes the following points:

1) Specific aim(s) of the lesson. Concentrate on one or two aims stated in behavioral terms.

2) Particular topic(s) for the day.

3) Brief outline of subject matter or listing of concepts or ideas to be involved in the day's instruction.

4) Teaching-learning activities to be employed in the achievement of the lesson's aim(s). It is helpful to note them opposite the subjects with which they are to be used.

5) Rough time budget. These are best put down in flexible terms, i.e., Discussion - 15-20 minutes.

6) Assignment. This involves the work to be completed by the learner by him/herself. It may need to be modified in the light of what took place during the class period.

7) Evaluation of lesson and suggestions. Such a section will allow you to react to what happened when the lesson plan was put into action for future reference. No lengthy analysis is needed and only a few words will serve to provide feedback for teaching the same ideas or subjects another time.

To help you organize your approach to short range planning the following form is offered as a suggestion you may find useful.

To conclude this chapter let me offer you a few ideas and cautions on the problems of instructional planning for inexperienced teachers.

1) Be as flexible as possible while still working toward your aims. The best laid plans of mice and men oft go astray and it is best to be ready for

SUBJECT _____ HOUR _____ DAY _____ DATE _____

DAILY LESSON PLAN

Unit Topic: _____

Topic(s) for today: _____

Aim(s) of lesson: _____

PROCEDURES

Ideas and Concepts to be Developed	Learning	Teaching	Time Budget

Evaluation and Suggestions:

Assignment:

problems.

2)   Have alternatives available if what you have planned simply does not

go.

3)   Do not pre-conceive what a particular class should be able to handle

during a given lesson and then proceed to jam it down their throats no matter

what happens. Adjust the amount of material to the ability of the class to

digest it properly. It is better to <u>teach</u> a little and do it well than to

<u>cover</u> a lot and do it poorly.

4)   Plan for much more than you think possible to teach in one class

period. As you start teaching it is likely that you will go through your

planned activities more rapidly than you anticipated. Beward of "running out

of gas" in the middle of the hour.

5)   Include a variety of activities in your plans. Be ready to change

when the class becomes bored or restless.

6)   Remember it often takes longer to complete most activities than

beginning teachers estimate.

7) Give learners time to learn in your time-budget. Points often must be re-made and once over an idea may not teach it.

8) Call attention by underlining in red those activities which must be included during that period, e.g., essential explanations, assignments, etc.

9) Plan in detail as you start your teaching. Many "on the spot" ideas come to the mind of an experienced teacher as he/she is instructing a class which do not occur to a neophite. "Off the cuff" teaching is best left until you have had some experience.

10) Keep in mind that the people you are teaching do not know the material. Begin simply and do not make assumptions about learner background unless you are sure of the facts.

As you can see, after reading this chapter, the actual teaching of a class is often the least time consuming element of instruction for the beginning teacher. It is the tip of the iceberg of which the part under the water is planning. There are few short cuts and you will find that your teaching will seldom rise above the level of your planning. If you want to teach well you must plan well.

CHAPTER 4

ORGANIZE YOUR INSTRUCTION FOR BEST RESULTS

One of the most important factors in effective teaching is how clearly the ideas to be learned are organized and structures. Studies in the psychology of learning have shown that people will generally comprehend things which have an organized pattern more easily than those which are disorganized. In this chapter we will consider some ways which will help you structure your teaching so that learners will increase achievement levels.

It is essential to remember the mind set (attitude toward learning the subject), the educational level and the maturity of your learning group as you organize your class work. Because you will know a good deal more about your subject than the class it is very easy to fall into two instructional errors.

1. Assume the learners know more about the subject matter than they actually do.

2. Skips steps in explanations thus losing the essential continuity of
a clear communication of ideas. The sensitive teacher constantly emphathizes
with classes in the effort to realize their learning problems.

The act of teaching involves breaking up large masses of ideas, subject
matter, skills, etc. into smaller, more digestable pieces and then arranging
them into an intelligible, logical sequence. In helping you to order your
teaching, I will deal with this matter under the three types of instructional
outcomes to be sought - understandings, skills and attitudes.

Teaching Understandings

In addressing this problem in relation to the area of understandings I
am going to suggest several steps.

Step I Know the learning skills and attitudes of your class. In academic
type situations the ability to read, write, think and discuss is important.
The level of these skills can be generally determined by talking with people
in the class, consulting previous academic records, if available, giving short
diagnostic tests and examining sample written work by learners.

Step II Complete a pre-instructional assessment of your pupils' knowledge of
the subject under consideration. This process does not need to be followed
for every lesson but is worthwhile when major new material is to be learned.
The means of securing this information is similar to that in Step I above.

Step III Connect new material with previously learned ideas or general knowledge. A review of prior learning or what is commonly known will provide a
platform upon which instruction can be built. You will be relating new and
strange ideas with old and familiar ones thus anchoring the superstructure to

a solid foundation.

Step IV Overview the subject to be studied. Point out briefly and generally

the main ideas involved and indicate the sequence to be followed. This will

answer the question, "What is to be done?"

Step V Make clear to the class the object of the teaching. Clarify the

objective(s) of the instruction so that everyone will know where it is moving.

Those aims must not be kept as secrets from the class by the instructor. This

will answer the question, "Why is this to be done?"

Step VI Explain the activities which learners and teacher will engage in to

achieve the aims of the study. This will give the class knowledge of what

will happen to them and helps relieve some learner apprehension. This answers

the question, "How?" Please note that Steps IV, V and VI above, the what, how

and why of teaching are applicable in two broad situations:

1) They apply to all types of instruction, not only that in the cognitive

or understand area.

2) They also are usable in teaching periods of varying length from the

daily lesson to the entire course. The time devoted to each step will depend on how large an instructional segment is under consideration. In the daily lesson only a few sentences will suffice but with units and courses more emphasis will be needed.

Step VII As you engage in teaching activities make sure to structure the approach to the subject matter in a logical and coherent manner, i.e. simple to complex, old to new, concrete to abstract, specific to general, etc. (or the reverse of these if it makes more sense).

Step VIII Organize your material into smaller sections. These small parts can usually be more easily understood by the average learner and can be more effectively handled by the teacher. (Caution: see Step IX as important to Step VIII.)

Step IX Integrate ideas as you teach them. They should be related to one another in the following ways.

Major points to general subject.

Major points to one another.

Smaller points to major points of which they are components.

Smaller points to one another.

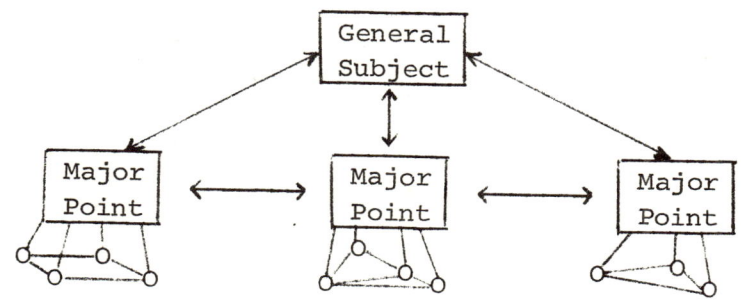

Step X Review main ideas and important points when needed. The old preacher put it well when, as he attempted to help a young minister put a sermon together, advised him to do it in three steps:

"Tell 'em what you are going to tell 'em.

Tell 'em.

Tell 'em what you told 'em."

Teaching Skills

We have considered teaching understandings now let us turn to the matter of organizing your approach to skills. This category involves both physical and mental skills and can be handled in "stages." The following suggestions will help you in dealing with this type of instruction.

Stage I. The learners must know why they are being asked to learn the skills. This realization will give some basic motivation to work on the skill as it can be seen as a necessary step in the larger process which is desired.

Stage II. Remember that skills begin as knowledge and these processes must first be carefully explained to the learner. Understanding should preceed practice.

Stage III. The skill should be broken into its component parts and placed in the proper sequence. The smaller sections can then be worked on separately and put together to form the complete skill.

Stage IV. Skills can be more quickly learned if they are demonstrated by the teacher or other qualified person.

Stage V. Often, if the skill is practiced at a slower pace as the learner begins the drills better understanding and mastery will result. After the basic pattern has been learned, it can be speeded up to an acceptable rate.

Stage VI. In general (a few exceptions exist) more effective skill learning will result if the practice periods are short. Extended drill sessions often reach the point of "diminishing returns" where boredom and fatigue reduce the effectiveness of the effort. For example, in studying the irregular verbs of a foreign language, four 15 minute drills are more efficient than one whole hour given to the same exercise.

Stage VII. Learners should practice skills at their own pace if at all possible. After the basic pattern has been clearly understood drill can well be carried on individually. People vary in their ability to do almost everything and the learning of skills is certainly no exception.

Stage VIII. Learners should be aware of their progress as they work on mastering the skill. Feedback and encouragement should be an integral part of skill teaching. Motivation will be heightened and a feeling of accomplishment will strengthen effort.

Stage IX. The skill, which has been practices in an artificial situation, should be put into practical application as soon as possible. Tennis backhand strokes learned by practice against a wall should be incorporated into a real game situation without delay.

These "stages" in skill instruction will not be applicable to every situation but the general pattern and sequence will be helpful in most cases. The skill of teaching skills has been outlined here. It is now up to you to practice until you are proficient.

Teaching Attitudes

The third area, in addition to understandings and skills, which should be dealt with in organizing instruction, is the matter of attitudes. In comparing the influence of rational thought to feeling, as motivators of human action, someone has put it thus, "Intellect is a mere speck afloat on a sea of emotion." We all know of its impact, the problem here is how to handle its instruction well.

Attitude formation goes on in _every_ education encounter. Each teacher influences the feelings of students and may not realize the extent and direction. How many teachers have taught learners to hate their subject, to be slipshod in work habits, to feel school is irrelevant or to be rude and impatient with others. The trick in teaching attitudes, of course, is to impart the _ones at which you are aiming_! This has proved so difficult to do that many teachers have simply given up trying and concentrate on skills and understandings only. Because it is hard to do does not make the accomplishment any less desirable.

Since attitudes are so crucial to every human activity some suggestions will now be offered to help you organize your instruction to create desirable attitudes in learners. The question obviously arises, "Which attitudes are 'desirable'?", and whose judgement is to be followed. Since we are concentrating on process in teaching and not substance this is not a problem we must solve. However, it can be said in passing that there is substantial agreement among well-intentioned, intelligent people on desirable attitudinal areas. To avoid any effort at teaching attitudes for fear of offending a few is a "cop out" of the first magnitude.

In dealing with the subject of teaching attitudes our consideration will be divided into two parts. First, some general principles of teacher attitude will be mentioned and second, instructional approaches will be suggested.

Let us begin by noting some ideas you should keep before you when teaching attitudes.

Idea I You should have clearly in mind the attitudes you wish learners to work toward before you begin instruction. Haphazard or incidental conception and planning will result in lack of direction and poor achievement.

Idea II Do not become discouraged if immediate and profound change does not take place in attitude growth. It often takes considerable periods of time to modify attitudes.

Idea III It is difficult (although by no means impossible) to measure real attitude change. Paper and pencil tests are not always valid, reliable instruments and personal observation of learners in actual life situations can be hard to manage.

Idea IV Set realistic goals without settling for too little. Consider the

37

type of learner with whom you are working, how much time you have and what you want to accomplish. Often we must be satisfied with small victories.

Idea V Avoid "preaching" at the class or constantly moralizing in attempts to inculcate attitudes. The desired attitude can and should be talked about but should not be "harped on." Also a superior, judgmental or patronizing stance by the teacher can result in reverse learning.

We will now turn our attention to setting up an organized approach to teaching attitudes. A number of "steps" will be offered for your consideration as you form your teaching style for attitudes.

Step I Determine the desired attitude changes in relation to currently held learner attitudes. Much unrealistic teaching and consequent frustration can be avoided by doing this. If you are not already acquainted with class attitude patterns pre-assessment processes such as discussions, pre-tests, etc. can be of assistance.

Step II Make clear to your class the nature of the desired attitudes so learners will know what you hope they will achieve. Too often classes remain in the dark regarding goals of learning especially in the matter of attitudes.

Step III Provide an information base of data about the attitude area. Changed thinking often begins with the acquisition of a sound factual foundation. This cannot be slanted or biased. No one likes to be manipulated and if "card-stacking" is observed by learners the whole effort can be jeopardized.

Step IV Provide a model of desirable attitude formation by someone the students can admire and with whom they can identify. An outstanding athlete enthusiastically endorsing worldwide human brotherhood can be a powerful incentive for imitation. Sometimes models are too far removed from the learners self-concept and an example in a more nearly similar situation will serve as a more powerful incentive. The visit to the class of a young girl who is coping successfully with blindness may provide a more realistic example of courage and perserverance to young people than stories about Helen Keller.

Remember you are a constant and immediate illustration of attitudes and "what you do speaks louder than what you say."

Step V Peer group and social group pressure are very influential in attitude formation. Group leaders can often show the way to others and it may be worthwhile to give special attention in this direction for support in attitude modification.

Step VI Enable learners to demonstrate the attitude toward which they are working. This can often be done only in a simulation or artificial situation, but it is a beginning. Experiences can be contrived in which students engage in role playing circumstances related to attitudinal learning.

Step VII Encouragement should be received by the learner on occasions in which worthwhile attitude change has been shown. Poor attitude patterns should be discouraged in appropriate ways. This positive reinforcement of desirable attitudinal change and inhibition of negative reaction should continue until the learners have established worthy standard of response.

This chapter has been concerned with helping you organize your instruction in an orderly, step-by-step fashion. The aim, as always, is greater clarity in your teaching resulting in increased learning by your class. Suggestions have been offered to aid you in so arranging your approaches to dealing with understandings, skills and attitudes that not only will comprehension be achieved but insight developed.

An _important caution_ must be given here. This book is _not_ a _recipe book_ and the ideas put forward here are guidelines not rigid, eternal, first principles. They should not be followed blindly but with sensitivity, modifying their application to the constantly changing conditions of all teaching - learning situations.

CHAPTER 5

INSTRUCTIONAL SKILLS YOU WILL NEED

Teaching has been characterized as, "an art based on scientific principles." Certainly a great deal of research has been done on teaching and learning. The wise person will profit from this storehouse of knowledge and not constantly bloody his/her head learning what is already known. Some however, will insist on "inventing the wheel" or "discovering fire," thus causing themselves pain and losing time in the process. There is wisdom in the expression, "Experience is the best teacher, but fools will have no other."

This chapter will be devoted to an explanation of a number of skills which the able teacher <u>not only knows</u> but <u>can employ with insight</u>. These skills have been identified as crucial to effective teaching by both extensive research on methods as well as the accumulated wisdom and experience of generations of teachers.

While you will amalgamate these skills into your total instructional technique, each one will do it in a slightly different way. The composite of your teaching skills, subject knowledge and personality has been labeled your "style." From the moment you start to teach you develop instructional habits which may remain with you for long periods of time. Be <u>very careful</u> to use good teaching skills <u>right from the start</u> so they will become habitual. It is much harder to break a bad pedagogical pattern than to learn to use the skill properly from the beginning.

With these cautions in mind, I hope you will examine the following teaching skills carefully. First understand the concept, then practice the skill and finally evaluate progress and practice again with changes if needed. This pattern should be continued until the skill has been mastered to the point desired. The order of listing here does not imply any relationship to the degree of importance.

Achieving Instructional Set

Any unit of instruction which is well begun is off to a sound start and is likely to have a good chance of achieving its goals. Simply stated this skill is what the teacher does to prepare the class for what is to be learned. Because we usually teach in daily lessons, instructional set most often takes place near the start of each period. It can and should be done whenever a new and significant idea is being considered. You would do it at the start of a course, a unit, a daily lesson or even a major concept within a lesson.

Gaining instructional set involves several processes which were mentioned in Chapter IV but, because of their importance will be sketched out briefly here once again.

1. Make clear to the class the subject matter, central ideas or main points to be dealt with in the time given for instruction. It is helpful to say it aloud and write it on the blackboard or otherwise identify it so that everyone will be clear on what is to be learned. If individuals have a sound notion of the subject matter they will be better able to master it than if they are not sure.

2. Identify the goals to be reached through the study being undertaken.

It <u>astounds me</u> that so often a group of learners approaches a subject without
realizing what they are aiming to know, be able to do, or feel. The teacher
so often keeps these objectives as a sort of secret from the class. Be sure
you tell your classes <u>why</u> they are studying the area and what they will derive
from the effort.

    3. Indicate the method(s) of instruction and how learning is to be accom-
plished. This will clarify to the class what will happen to them and what they
will be asked to do in the process of learning. Knowing this will help students prepare themselves mentally and emotionally for the activities to be
undertaken.

    These three points mentioned above can be condensed into three words.
They will signify the ideas presented here and hopefully remind you not to
forget to insure your classes always know the "What", "Why" and "How" of your
teaching.

    4. Establish a favorable attitude in the minds of the learners toward

the subject and activities involved. This can be done through arousing the interest of the students or emphasizing the importance of the material to be learned. Catching the interest of a class can be done in many ways - telling subject-related anecdotes, asking thought-provoking questions, taking an extreme position on the issue to be studied, connecting material to be covered with a current event or to the lives and experiences of the learners. If such an "interest catching device" cannot be found at least an indication of the subject's importance and worth should be stressed. When a subject is neither interesting nor important learners will wonder why you are teaching it.

5. Connect the new material to be learned with what has been previously taught or to general knowledge. When a class can see the relationships between strange or unfamiliar ideas and something they already know the attachment and retention will be stronger and longer-lasting. It is wise to first review the previously learned material to bring it to the minds of the students once again. Then new ideas can be shown in their relationship with the old and the connection made firm.

Obtaining Closure

If achieving instructional set is accomplished at the beginning of teaching a course, unit, lesson, or idea, closure is what takes place at the end of such a teaching cycle. It simply involves bringing the considerations of the idea or subject to a meaningful close. In doing this you will take several steps.

1. Re-emphasize the main ideas which have been stressed as a part of the learning process which has (hopefully) taken place. There is often a problem

in remembering these points made during a lecture, discussion, explanation, demonstration, etc. To help with this difficulty it is wise to put such central ideas on the blackboard as you mention them. It will then be a simple matter to note them as you work on closure.

2. Relate these important concepts with what will be studied next in class. This integration will point out relationships which can assist in perception and understanding. The teacher may say something like this: "So far we have learned this, this and this. Now we will go a step further tomorrow and see that..."

3. Give the learners a feeling of achievement. When individuals feel progress is being made and success gained, the motivational drive will show itself more strongly. This encouragement is often given to groups more than individuals. It tends to leave the learners with a positive feeling toward the subject and the instructional act, and will help them take up the learning task more willingly next time. It can be phrased so class members feel they understand some ideas they did not know at the beginning of the learning period. For example, "It seems we are not aware of several things about_____that we didn't realize an hour ago."

Reinforcement   (Group and Individual)

This is a process which aims at strengthening worthwhile responses in learners and reducing or eliminating those which are not desirable. The strengthening aspect is often referred to as "positive reinforcement" and the eliminating kind as "negative reinforcement." It is a way of conditioning people to do things they should and refrain from what they should not do. It involves a system of rewards and punishments which, when offered in conjunction with actions either helps or fix or extinguish that response in the mind of the learner. It is outside the satisfaction someone receives when he/she has reached self-set goals. For the most part you as teacher will provide these reactions to student activity in the form of rewards or punishments. These can range from very mild to unusually strong and it is necessary to use them in an intelligent and sensitive manner to achieve maximum results.

Listed below are some important ideas you should consider carefully if you wish to use this teaching skill effectively.

1. Remember to encourage the group as well as the individual for work well done. It helps form an espirit de corps and stimulates cooperative effort.

2. Underplay positive reinforcement somewhat. Do not gush forth superlatives for every action as it diminishes the worth of real compliments and often embarrasses the learner if overdone.

3. Come across as absolutely genuine and sincere in your positive reinforcement. Unless you are exceptionally clever in this matter you may impress your class as phoney and artificial with only the desire to manipulate them.

Keep in mind that there are many things you can be really pleased about regarding class or individual performance if you don't set your expectation levels at unrealistic levels.

4. You can compliment progress as well as absolute achievement. If the results of learner effort are not, in themselves, of high quality at least growth toward objectives can be encouraged.

5. Avoid falling into a rut of routine reinforcement techniques. Some teachers utter the same word or phrase constantly so that it becomes virtually meaningless. Thus a "good" from the teacher which might have had some impact the first few times, quickly tails off to be no more effective than a sneeze or cough in motivating behavior. Reinforcement, to work well, should be varied in terms of who is involved, how it is handled, what is encouraged to discouraged and when it is done.

6. Remember encouragement has been found to be a more potent force in shaping worthwhile student behavior than punishment. This certainly does not mean negative reinforcement should always be avoided, but in the words of the old song you should, "accentuate the positive!"

7. Suit the level of praise to the nature of the effort and the ability of the group or individual. A routine response from a very bright student should not elicit the same teacher reaction as a great try from the slowest person in class.

8. Among many means of reinforcing student behavior the following can be noted.

A. Written comments by the teacher on papers and tests.

B. Verbal encouragement.
C. Simply calling students by their names.
D. Looking pleasantly at your learners.
E. Smiling.
F. Nodding your head.
G. Gesturing.
H. Writing student response on board.
I. Repeating learner contributions with obvious pleasure.
J. Others you will discover for yourself.

Reinforcement is a teaching skill which, when used sincerely and skillfully, will show surprising power in creating desirable learning attitudes.

Feedback

It is necessary for you as teacher to know the extent to which learners understand what is being taught. The process by which the knowledge is received is called feedback. Without it an instructor is unable to handle such important matters as adjusting the rate of teaching, knowing whether or not to give additional examples, recognizing when to simplify ideas, appreciating the need to go over a point again or understanding when to leave a topic. The skilled teacher builds into plans provisions for feedback and will employ a variety of means to gather this information. He/she thus will be enabled to modify class procedures to suit the existing learning situation. It is analogous to a ship's captain taking constant depth soundings while passing through a treacherous channel.

What are some ways to understand the learners grasp of the material being taught?

1. Observe the faces of your learners - are they bored, confused, inattentive?

2. Ask students questions about what is being presented. Do not be

<u>satisfied</u> with an "Are there any questions?" approach to the problem. Often a few of the bright students will nod their heads and the teacher may feel the whole class has grasped a concept when such is not the case at all.

3. Ask if anyone can re-explain what you have just tried to make clear. It could be a real eye-opener to you.

4. Give a short written quiz on the subject being taught. Often such tests are not marked but served only to provide information to both teacher and learners.

5. Examine the work being done by your class as it relates to the matters being taught.

6. Request the students to give examples of the ideas being presented. These applications of concepts by your learners can furnish a good insight into the level of understanding reached.

The problem of feedback is not quite so much how to obtain it as remembering to do it at all. Many beginners plunge on blindly without feedback only to discover, too late, that what they had assumed was being comprehended had not been understood at all.

Focusing

One requirement in effective instruction is to emphasize those things which are important over those which are not so crucial. You, as the teacher, realize which points are most significant because of your broad background in the subject. Learners are without this knowledge and so it is your responsibility to provide this stress. Such structuring of major and minor ideas will give your students an idea of the organization and relationship of the material to be learned. Some suggestions on focusing will now be offered to which you will be able to add your own ideas.

1. You can simply say, "This is important, remember it."

2. The point can be written on the blackboard or overhead transparency.

3. It can be repeated for emphasis.

4. Students can be asked to write the idea in a notebook.

5. Examples can be given to clarify and demonstrate the worth of the concept.

6. The amount of time spent on the matter is often an indicator of importance.

7. Others you will think of yourself.

Style Variation

If variety is the "spice of life" it could be called "the perfume of teaching." It adds interest and style to an art which can become very dull and boring to learners. The thrust should be to avoid boredom because it inhibits learning and reduces retention. The temptation is strong to settle into a pleasant "fur-lined rut" after a period of teaching. Teachers often tend to feel that everyone learns in the pattern which appealed to them as students. Many ways to vary teaching style will occur to those who are sensitive to the problem. A few ideas are offered here as a start.

1. Movement. There is a dichotomy of "feast or famine" in this connection. Some instructors are so lethargic that they stand, or worse sit, in one place scarcely blinking their eyes. Others race around the room in a frenzy of activity which arouses either exhaustion or tension in their listeners. The "golden mean" is to seek enough movement to show vitality and help interest the class but not so much as to induce nervous prostration.

2. Gesturing. This can add life, emphasis and meaning to the oral communication of the teacher. Phrenetic gesturing becomes nerve wracking, so again a sane middle ground must be found between "the statue" and "the perpetual movement machine."

3. Interaction Styles. Between the two types of people in a typical formal learning situation at least three patterns of relationship are possible. The teacher to an individual student is one, the teacher to total group is another and student(s) to student(s) is a third. Using all of these options can add needed variety to a learning situation.

4. Pausing. This must be used with caution, but when it is a slight pause can be effective. It can signal to the class the approach of an important point. It may be employed to gain the students attention or indicate a

switch to another topic. Too many pauses result in a jerky presentation and overlong pauses encourage learner boredom and opens up the potention for disruption. Short verbal pauses may help you appear more fluent and dynamic in speaking. It is wise to train yourself to avoid the "uhms", "ok's", "ahs" and other "verbal spacers" which are commonplace with those inexperienced in front of groups. They can be replaced by a simple short period of silence while you collect your thoughts for the next statement.

5. Switching Sensory Channels. Everyone learns best in slightly differing ways. Therefore the sense entry into each person's consciousness will vary in effectiveness depending on the individual. To some the visual impact carries more force than with others. This applies to the other senses as well. For this reason, it is wise to use several sensory inputs in attempting to reach learners. Generally the more senses employed the greater the effect on learning there will be. An example in earth science shows how this idea can be applied. If a class is studying about how to identify types of rocks it would be helpful if the teacher not only talked about the subject, showed pictures, and drew diagrams on the board, but had rock samples which could be hefted and smelled for identifying characteristics.

What I have presented here are only some of the many ideas you can use to add variety to your teaching style. Your efforts in this matter will be well repaid by more effectiveness in teaching and thereby learning as well.

This chapter has highlighted some crucial instructional skills which you will, hopefully, want to incorporate into your "teaching style." Exactly how you accomplish this will be an individual matter for you to decide. It will, however, <u>need practice</u> as you probably will not be able to command many of these skills on a professional level as you begin your teaching. Consult Chapter I, "Learning How To Teach", on feedback devices you can use to test your performance and increase your ability to use these skills effectively.

CHAPTER 6

HOW TO HANDLE BASIC TEACHING METHODS

The number of instructional approaches used by teachers is virtually unlimited when you consider the variations and combinations possible under different circumstances and the diversity of individuals involved. When these techniques are simplified and distilled to their essential substance, however, only a few fundamental methods remain. They revolve about three general types of activities:

1. Information receiving

2. Thinking and analyzing

3. Applying and practicing

In this chapter we will deal with two basic teaching methods related to the first two activities mentioned above. The matter of "applying and practicing" has been covered in Chapter IV in the section on skills and will not be repeated here. The instructional approaches included are:

Explanations and lectures

Discussions

It will be clear to you, if you think about the matter, that there are many ways of acquiring an information base besides listening to a lecture or explanation. One obvious method would be from reading material about the subject. It is the object of this book, however, to help to do those things which only a teacher does and therefore the concentration will be on the oral, information giving presentation. A variety of teaching techniques can also be used in dealing with the second category, thinking and analyzing. Here again other approaches suggest themselves but since, as a discussion leader you are so directly involved we will center on that process.

The Lecture

We will define the lecture here in very broad terms as any instructional talk or explanation given to a group of learners. It is probably the most widely used instructional activity used by teachers. It may also be the most misused, abused and overused teaching technique. This does not, however, keep it from being a splendid teaching tool when skillfully used on appropriate occasions. I want to suggest to you now several ideas which can help you refine your lecture into an effective method of teaching.

Lecture Idea I. The lecture can be used as a time-saving method of passing on to learners needed information and data. Several points should be remembered when doing this:

A. Do not repeat what learners have already read unless it requires some interpretation or clarification.

B. You can condense material which would take your class a long time to acquire.

C. You can simplify complicated ideas which the learner would have difficulty understanding when working on his/her own.

Lecture Idea II. The lecture may well be employed to analyze, compare, apply and evaluate factual material the class has accumulated. In this process the teacher must deal with ideas, issues, concepts and principles primarily, while constantly using data, facts and logic to buttress and substantiate assertions. You will thus serve as a model for students as they learn to bring information to bear on analyzing problems and dealing with issues.

Lecture Idea III. Lectures should be used only when they are the most appropriate method of instruction available NOT the most convenient. Lecturing is often the easiest way out but not necessarily the most effective teaching activity. You should first consult your objective, then determine the best approach to use, not visa versa.

Lecture Idea IV. Lecturing can well be used for several purposes:

    A. To arouse interest in a topic.
    B. To pass along unique experiences you have had which will enhance
        learner understanding.
    C. To introduce a new topic or unit to the class.
    D. To summarize or review a topic or unit which your class has studied.
    E. Help learners acquire needed information not otherwise available.
    F. Others depending upon circumstances.

Lecture Idea V. The wise lecturer seeks constant feedback from his/her audience on how well the material is being understood. Feedback techniques were discussed in Chapter V and hopefully you will practice them as you lecture.

Most important, you must accommodate what you do in the light of feedback you receive. If ideas are not clear they must be re-explained, additional examples provided and whatever action is needed to clarify misconceptions must be taken.

Lecture Idea VI. The lecture techniques and length of presentation must be suited to the nature of the learners involved. The younger or less verbal the group - the shorter, more concrete, more interesting the talk should be. After some contact with your students you will be able to make decisions on the length and methods to be used.

<u>Lecture Idea VII</u>. Organize and structure the ideas in your lecture so that the <u>learner</u>, being unacquainted with the topic, can understand the points and perceive their relationships. (Refer back to Chapter IV).

<u>Lecture Idea VIII</u>. Teach your listeners the "learning skill" of taking notes from a lecture. This will involve another sensory input to the consciousness of the learner beside the hearing of the words and seeing the speaker with any A.V. aids which might be used. This kinesthetic sense of writing can increase the understanding and retention of ideas. A few suggestions may help you teach note-taking.

A. Be very organized in your lecture so it will be easy to follow.
B. Hand out a partially completed sheet of notes for the lecture with some points (major and minor) left out so that the listener must pick them up from your talk.
C. Review basic topical outlining with your class.
D. Stress the use of abbreviations.
E. Urge students to put ideas in their own words.
F. You can demonstrate note-taking by doing it yourself on the board (or overhead transparency) from a lecture you have taped yourself.
G. Speak distinctly and slowly enough to be easily understood.
H. Examine notes of learners and re-teach when necessary.

<u>Lecture Idea IX</u>. Illustrate the ideas in your lecture through the use of examples. By doing this you show how the elements in the concept are incorporated in a practical situation. A <u>major problem</u> in using examples and illustrations is that listeners may not perceive the relationship between the principle and the example. You must often point this out and note the elements they have in common. It is very helpful to provide a second illustration of the same principle since the application may not be clear from the first example. Additional instances can be sought from learners to further fix the idea and provide more feedback.

Lecture Idea X. Be very conscious of your vocabularly loading. Lecturing

must be a process of communicating ideas. When words are used which have no

definite meaning to your listeners ideas cannot pass from your mind to the

minds of the learners. Much teaching of new material involves fixing the

meaning of terms which signify concepts and ideas. The following suggestions

may help you deal with this problem.

   A. Be careful to insure that a majority of the words you use are likely

to be known to your listeners.

   B. Do not "talk down" or patronize your audience with a "baby talk"

attitude.

   C. Define new or complicated terms with the feelings of your listeners

in mind. Such phrases as, "Let us remind ourselves of what this means," or

"You may recall that...means..." are some samples of this sensitivity.

   D. Use new or complex words in a context which will allow learners to deduce the meaning from other words in the sentence.

E. Supply a synonym immediately following a new word to help show its meaning. For example, "He was the master of hyperbole, exaggeration".

Lecture Idea XI. Supplement the spoken word of a lecture with other audio-visual entries into the learners consciousness. Since this is covered in the next chapter I will just say that this process not only aids in clarifying meanings but helps to avoid boredom by adding variety to the presentation.

Lecture Idea XII. Use notes within reason. On the one hand you cannot memorize your lecture but on the other you should not read it either. A brief outline, which can be followed at a glance as you lecture, will enable you to structure meaning and avoid forgetting important points.

Lecture Idea XIII. How you speak can be as important as what you say. We have all heard some profound remarks uttered in such a monotonous manner, or in swallowed words that their worth was almost completely lost. It can also be a common experience to hear words of doubtful truth or value delivered with such force and dynamism that they are nearly believable. There follow here some useful speaking techniques which can assist you to avoid problems common to almost every beginning lecturer.

A. Use good intonation. Avoid speaking on the same pitch. Varying the tone by raising two steps above and two below normal will provide interest in your delivery.

B. Speak with different levels of force or intensity. Some ideas can be well expressed in quite a matter of fact voice, but others should be uttered with more thrust to add impact and importance.

C. Speak loudly enough so that <u>everyone</u> in the room can easily hear you. Too much volume, however, can be as bad as not enough and may result in nervous tension among your listeners. Do not try to outshout a noisy class - your voice will usually not last. Remember to get plenty of air in your lungs, project your voice, open your mouth to allow the sound out and be careful to enunciate your words clearly. Mumbling inhibits communication.

D. Speak to your listeners at a pace brisk enough to maintain interest and attention, but not so rapidly that they cannot follow you. More beginning teachers speak too quickly than too slowly.

E. Look at your learners as you speak to them as it will enhance your lecture in several ways. First, it will provide dynamism and personal intensity to what you are saying, second it indicates your interest in what you are talking about and third it helps control "restless learners". Some starting teachers have difficulty in "meeting the eyes" of large groups of students. A little trick may help you. Look them "in the nose" or "in the forehead".

This provides the same effect and you will soon be able to meet their eyes after a bit of experience. Make sure to look over the whole class and avoid teaching too much to one part of the room.

F. Avoid nerve-wracking mannerisms as you speak. This includes "verbal spacers", previously referred to, as well as pet phrases repeated constantly. In addition physical and facial mannerisms can be distracting.

The suggestions on lecturing offered here are by no means a complete coverage but they do represent a very good beginning. The big problem is to obtain adequate feedback so you can identify your personal problems in lecturing. My suggestion, to repeat what was mentioned in Chapter I, is to use both audio tapes and video tapes made of yourself as you communicate with your class. Nothing will give you a clearer, more honest picture of your strengths and weaknesses. It does take courage though!

The Discussion

The term "discussion" has been used to cover a wide variety of activities. For this reason we had better define what is meant by the word at the start of this section. Discussion involves verbal interchange among a group of participants, dealing with a specific topic or problem, seeking through an exchange of ideas to arrive at a better understanding of the subject. It has been referred to also as "group thinking about an issue".

So much for what it is. What isn't it? It is not brainstorming, although sometimes that process can very well play a part in real discussion. Neither is it a "bull session" in which any subject is legitimate and often the central ideas shift rapidly from topic to topic. Discussion is also not a recitation, which is really nothing more than an oral test. Here again, however, this method of supplying factual support is fundamental to the consideration of any issue. You can appreciate that what you may have experienced as "discussion" in your own learning background may have been something else.

The skillful handling of discussion is among the most demanding and involved of all teaching techniques. You should not avoid learning to do it well since it can be the vehicle by which some of the most valuable educational goals can be achieved.

At the pinnacle of its effectiveness discussion can help your students to learn how to think. Properly handled this instructional method can assist in giving learners experience in such higher mental processes as application, analysis, synthesis and evaluation. Any activity which results in such worthwhile end products is surely worth your strenuous efforts.

If, at this point, you realize that you do not know much about leading a real discussion another problem will emerge clearly. Your learners will hardly ever know how to engage in meaningful discussion. Despite this many teachers assume that their classes have somehow acquired discussion skills as they have progressed through life and/or formal education.

The remaining part of this chapter will deal with two main subjects. First, how to help your students learn to handle both controversial issues and discussion roles. Second, how you, as a leader, can function so that the process will be one of learning and not simply "an exchange of prejudices or ignorances." The following suggestions are offered as guidelines for sound discussion.

<u>Discussion Point I. Teach your learners how to cope with controversial</u>

<u>issues</u>. These, of course, are topics which are open to more than one informed

opinion. Hardly any general subject area is entirely without issues which

arouse substantial differences of opinion. In order to <u>learn</u> from discussing

such matters rather than simply <u>argue</u> about them your classes must be prepared

to handle them properly. You can do this by insuring that your learners are

equipped to deal with the following principles.

1. The discussants must realize clearly what the topic is.

2. They must have an adequate information base about the subject.

3. The discussion group should understand "suspended judgement" as a

concept, and be able to practice it.

4. Learners need to recognize biased opinions and how they can be iden-

tified from such clues as wording of opinion, place occupied by the holder of

the opinion, appeals to the emotions, etc.

5. In building their own opinions students must be taught to refer to

facts, sound logic and authorative source.

6. They must allow others the same right to freedom of opinion and ex-

pression they want for themselves.

7. The individuals learning to discuss should appreciate the possibilities

of several "truths" emerging from the discussion.

8. All participants will need to practice the art of <u>real</u> listening to

the opinions of others, especially if they differ from one another.

How you will teach these skills will depend on circumstances. It may be

helpful to mount a two pronged attack on the problem. One prong could be a

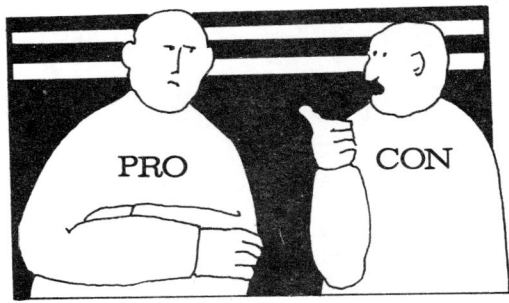

study of the concept through reading, lecture, etc. A second approach would

involve providing actual examples of confronting controversial issues. A

discussion of such a subject can be carried on for the class by several

teachers or other qualified persons. This would furnish a model of process

and attitude for student imitation.

Discussion Point II. Instruct your classes how to assume various roles

in a discussion. To make discussion worth the work involved, learners must

realize the processes which take place and their function as participants.

A successful discussion depends heavily upon student knowledge and competency

in both group and individual responsibilities so students must be trained to

handle them well. In order to really become a part of class operation these

skills must be identified, analyzed and practiced. After explaining the vari-

ous roles to your group, experience in handling them must be gained. One

method of doing this is to make up cards designating the individual to play a

particular role for one discussion. These cards would be rotated until a vari-

ety of roles has been assumed by all learners. The part played by each of the following roles should be clear to all:

1. Question raiser

2. Information supplier

3. Clarifier

4. Integrater

5. Reinforcer

6. Tension reliever

7. Focuser on subject

8. Summarizer

Of course your students should understand in a real discussion that they will undertake several roles and not be restricted to one only. When they master the fundamentals of these skills, the discussions in your classes will assume a quality which will happily surprise you.

Discussion Point III. You must understand and be able to use discussion leadership skills. While on some occasions learners will be leaders of discussion in your classes, for the most part this task will fall to you. In this section several of these functions will be identified and briefly explained. You should be prepared to handle them smoothly and skillfully so that the discussions will proceed well.

Skill I. Introduce the subject. It will assist the process if you provide a general introduction on the topic involved. You can do this in several ways:

1. Clearly delineate the issue, question, or problem to be discussed. (You will often select the subject yourself - make sure it is worthwhile,

interesting and "discussable".)

2. Create interest in the topic.

3. Provide some background information or a framework to begin consideration of the issue. It is frequently worthwhile to talk briefly about the broad area then focus in on the part which will be of interest for the discussion.

4. Relate the topic to what has been previously learned in the course or to what is general knowledge.

Skill II. Establish classroom atmosphere favorable to discussion. This is crucial to widespread participation and its achievement usually depends upon your sensitivity and skill as a leader. It can be encouraged by these actions:

1. Show a real interest in the learners ideas and contributions.

2. Provide appropriate and meaningful reinforcement of student efforts (both group and individual).

3. Manifest friendliness to the class as a whole and individuals as well.

4. Avoid a show of impatience or boredom with student contributions.

5. Guard against expressions of ridicule or sarcasm in relation to honestly expressed learner opinion even if biased or uninformed.

Skill III. Develop skill as a questioner. Good questions not only form the thrust of a discussion and are indispensible to its success. They have the qualities of clarity, of being appropriate to the discussants level of understanding, and requiring thought of answer. Some brief suggestions follow here which may help you develop your own "questioning style."

1. Avoid asking the obvious question. The "Who's buried in Grant's

tomb?" type query may insult or embarrass your class.

2. Point your questions adequately. The "What about Russia?" item is so vague as to be difficult to deal with properly.

3. Emphasize "higher order questions" (those which require more mental effort than the simple recall of facts - the "Why", "How", type). You certainly will not neglect the "lower order questions", (the "What", "Where", "When" variety) so often needed to fix a factual base for dealing with issues. The main reason for a discussion however, remains to employ the higher mental processes of analysis, application, comparison, synthesis, etc. in considering principles, concepts and issues.

4. Suit your questions to a variety of learner abilities - some which can be handled by less able students, others by the brighter ones.

5. Frame your questions in as short, direct and understandable terms as possible. If students cannot respond to an inquiry it should be because they do not know the answer rather than inability to discover the meaning of the question.

6. Write out a number of major questions and place them in a logical sequence before the discussion begins. This will help eliminate forgetting worthwhile items. You will find that from each large question many smaller, more specific inquiries will grow naturally.

Skill IV. Integrate and structure the discussion as it progresses. Unless you, as leader, relate the points made by the participants with the major topic and also with other student contributions the result may be a hodgepodge. This integration and structuring usually cannot be done by implication. It must be overt and obvious. The _blackboard_ is a useful ally in emphasizing these relationships.

Skill V. _Draw as many learners into the discussion as possible._ How well you succeed in this often depends on such factors as the type of class atmosphere, the interest of the subject, the nature of the questions and the difficulty level of the issue being considered. You may be able to involve students by suiting questions to their ability and interest areas. Shy students can be encouraged through gentle questioning but often they would rather die than answer. Use judgement in pressing them. In many cases, however, it is surprising to find they are following the discussion closely without actually speaking. A realistic and acceptable goal for actual class participation would involve between two thirds and three fourths of those present.

Skill VI. _Learn some techniques of starting a group to discuss._ There are a number of actions you can take to get a discussion moving:

1. Select an interesting, worthwhile and appropriate topic.

2. Provide an introduction - a lead in - set the stage - for the discussion.

3. Begin with some provocative or controversial questions.

4. Act as the "Devil's Advocate" by taking an extreme position and defending it. Be sure students realize the falacy of the stand before you leave the subject.

5. Use "buzz group" or "Phillips 66" procedures. This involves breaking a larger group into smaller parts of perhaps 6 people each. Every minor section is given the same topic to talk over and the results are brought back to the main group. The time for this process is short, varying from 5-15 minutes

generally. Shy students feel more comfortable in this setting and divergent small group conclusions often stimulate more active large group discussions as it comes together once again.

Skill VII. Handle non-response problems with insight. When you ask questions in a discussion you may not receive any response. Consider the following ideas in dealing with the problem.

1. You may have asked too difficult a question - simplify it.

2. Your question may have been too easy - make it more rigorous so as not to insult your class.

3. Throw out your question to the whole class to encourage everyone to think of the answer. After this an individual may be specified to respond.

4. If no immediate reaction is forthcoming be patient and wait a bit - thought may be going on. Judgement must be used in this so do not wait too long.

5. Avoid jumping from student to student for an answer with a more desperate tone in your voice with each move.

6. Rephrase your question. It is quite possible that what is crystal-clear to you is very muddy to learners.

7. Provide a hint or two as to the answer for a difficult question. This can help if only a brief nudge is needed, but can become cumbersome if taken to extremes.

8. Realize your class may simply not be ready for discussion of the topic. They might not know enough basic information to even attempt to discuss and it is foolish to "try to get blood from a stone."

Skill VIII. <u>Summarize and review at the end of a discussion</u>. This is <u>often not done</u> and for good reason - it can be difficult. The process is so worthwhile, however, in fixing in the minds of your learners the main ideas and conclusions reached by the group that it is imperative you learn to do it. Two actions should be taken:

1. <u>Remember to do it</u>. Allow a few minutes at the end of the allotted time period as it may be the most important thing you will do. Students can often help in summaries if alerted beforehand.

2. Put main ideas on the blackboard or overhead projector <u>as they are made</u> through the discussion. Doing this not only helps you summarize at the end but allows learners to note the points which have been made and understand the relationship among the ideas expressed.

Now...after reading this material you <u>know</u> a considerable amount about teaching via the lecture and discussion methods. This, of course, is <u>not enough</u>, you must <u>practice</u> these skills and refine your techniques so that you are <u>comfortable</u> with them and <u>effective</u> in their use. Only then will they truly become part of your own personal "teaching style".

CHAPTER 7

HOW TO ACHIEVE CLARITY IN TEACHING

It is obvious that an essential requisite of successful teaching and learning is clear communication. This is one of the central tasks of every instructor and the extent of your achievement will depend in large part on how effectively you transmit the ideas to be learned to your class. Many people attempting to teach others are frustrated because little or no learning takes place. They do not seem to realize that a primary reason for this is that what is being presented is not clear or intelligible to those who are to learn.

This chapter will present a number of ideas designated to help you achieve clarity in your instruction. They are not offered in any order of importance but with the idea that all contribute to the goal of clear, understandable teaching. If you know them and appreciate their worth you will incorporate the concepts into your own personal teaching style. You will thus, hopefully, become an instructor whose classes will be noted for their clearness and learner understanding. In some cases these principles will have been mentioned in another connection on preceding pages. Nevertheless they have an application to the subject of clarity and will therefore be included here as a review of essential concepts.

Clarity Idea I. Make clear to your class the goals of instruction. This step should be taken at every stage from objectives for the whole course to what is to be learned in a single lesson. Make sure this is really compre-

hended. Too many teachers keep the learning aims a kind of secret known only

to themselves and hardly ever shared with the people most affected.

Clarity Idea II. Empathize with your learners background, feelings and

interests. Put yourself in the place of those in your class and look at the

material and teaching methods from their point of view. If you do this hon-

estly it will give you worthwhile insights into how to be more effective in

your instruction. One of the best ways to do this is to make up a "personal

data sheet" containing information about each person in the group. Without

becoming too personal you can ask about each learners educational experience,

interests, work situation (if any), something of the home background, without

prying, and other information you think appropriate. The answers will help

you understand the individuals in your class more completely and thus enable

you to teach them with more insight.

Clarity Idea III. Do not assume too much knowledge on the part of your

learners. Beginning teachers often make assumptions that their classes know

more about the material to be studied than is warranted. As a result planning

is faulty and teacher discouragement ensues. (See Clarity Idea IV for help.)

Clarity Idea IV. Use pre-assessment devices to understand student know-

ledge as you begin teaching new material. The wise teacher will "test the

water" before jumping into instructional procedures beyond the depth of the

learners. Such techniques as questioning, pre-instructional diagnostic tests,

discussions of the general subject etc., can aid you in finding out where your

class is in their knowledge. You can thus start at a point which will not lose students by beginning on too advanced a level, or bore your class by commencing at too elementary a level.

Clarity Idea V. Teach in steps short enough to avoid unduly taxing the learners ability to comprehend. In other words, do not try to cover too much material in "one bite". Break it up into "digestible pieces".

Clarity Idea VI. Relate new ideas to what students already know. You can provide connections with what has previously been learned in your class or what is general knowledge. This can be accomplished by pointing out similarities and differences between new and known material, trends can be shown, continuation of processes or application of ideas brought out to clarify the relationship between the new and old.

Clarity Idea VII. Suit your vocabularly to the learners level of understanding. Words are tools which transfer ideas from the mind of one person to that of another. Unless words are understood to mean pretty much the same thing to both people real communication will be difficult or impossible. One of the great sins of teaching is "verbalism" or the use of words not comprehended by the listener. Be sure to make use of feedback devices to determine if your words are being understood.

Clarity Idea VIII. Employ a variety of teaching-learning approaches. Most teaching is done with groups of more than one person. We know that individuals learn in different ways, at varying rates and through diverse media. One student may comprehend best through reading, another by hearing still another by writing. We also realize that the impact on understanding is generally increased through using more than one sense entry into the consciousness.

The implications are obvious. The use of different teaching-learning methods
and media will accommodate the diversity of learning patterns commonly found
in students.

Clarity Idea IX. Make use of examples and illustrations to show meaning.
The enunciation of a concept or principle verbally or in print does not insure
its understanding. If you can show how the idea works in practice or give an
instance of its application in a particular situation clarity will be increased.

Clarity Idea X. Preview what is to be learned. When you briefly sketch
the material to be presented prior to the actual instruction you furnish a
needed introduction for those to whom the ideas are unfamiliar. This provides
perspective and shows relationship among the various components involved.

Clarity Idea XI. Emphasize important ideas. People who are not acquainted
with a subject will often not be able to identify which points are of primary
significance from those of secondary or tertiary importance. It is your responsibility to do this for your class.

Clarity Idea XII. Integrate and relate what is to be learned. Point out clearly how each concept fits into a general framework or system. Make sure there are bridges which connect ideas with one another so that they are not simply little islands of information floating free and unrelated.

Clarity Idea XIII. Follow a step-by-step approach in explaining. In most instances you will want to proceed in a logical sequence, i.e., from the simple to the complex, the concrete to the abstract, the practical to the theoretical, etc. In some cases you will wish to reverse this order. At any rate, go a step at a time and do not leave out steps in any explanation. Taking such a short-cut may reduce instruction time but often requires re-explaining later.

Clarity Idea XIV. Use feedback devices to determine the extent of learner comprehension. You cannot teach clearly if you do not know how much the students are grasping of what they are studying. In this regard be sure to use adequate feedback testing and do not delude yourself on the level of achievement by always taking the positive indications and ignoring the negative one.

Clarity Idea XV. Insure the learning materials are suitable for your class. The most common learning materials are printed ones. To be effective they must be matched to your classes ability to assimilate them. It will help to know the reading levels of your learners and the graded levels of the material you are giving them. Besides consulting reading test scores, however, you can judge the appropriateness of printed sources by your own quizzes, discussions and informal questioning.

A quick and quite usable method to determine the reading difficulty of any printed material is the following index:

Select a passage (even better two passages and run the test twice) of about 100 words from the books being used. It could be slightly larger - 101-2 or 3 words but the articles "a", "an" and "the" should not be included in this count. From this section you must find out two figures.

1. P.W. or the number of polysyllabic words - those with three or more syllables in them. (Do not include words which are mode polysyllabic by the addition of "es" or "ed".)

2. S.L. or the average sentence length in the selection of 100 words. Count the total number of words (not including "ands", "the's" and "a's") and divide by the number of sentences for S.L.

Then put these items into the following formula:

P.W. + S.L. x .4 = approximate reading grade level.

Similar care should be exercised in selecting all the material you ask your class to use in the learning process.

Clarity Idea XVI. Whether using deductive or inductive approaches to teaching, organization is necessary. The deductive method is simply a process in which a principle, idea or concept is assumed to be correct and applications of it are made to particular situations or examples cited to demonstrate how the idea works. It proceeds from the general concept to the specifics of how it is applied. In using this approach you must be sure learners understand how an application shows the working of the principle. The elements held in common between the idea and the example may need to be pointed out to make clear the relationship.

The inductive approach is the reverse of the deductive. This method moves from the specific to the general, from the applications and examples to the principle involved. Here the learners identify the common elements in several illustrations and form a generalization or concept. While the inductive method usually requires more student thinking it also involves two hazards. First, more time is consumed in this process and if rushed often does not work properly. Second, when learners are unable to see the common elements in the examples the teacher makes the generalization. In this way the essence of method is greatly lessened in value.

Some learning situations, however, are tailor-made for one technique or the other. You must use your own judgement as to which would be most appropriate. Do avoid settling into a rut and depending on one constantly.

Clarity Idea XVII. Make sure your learners have the skills needed to engage in the activities you are providing. Examine your assumptions about student abilities to handle the level of reading required, their listening and note taking skills, their knowledge of how to locate information, to write and to discuss with insight. These general abilities must be coupled with the specific skills needed for the study of a particular topic.

Clarity Idea XVIII. Re-teach when necessary. Not only should you recognize that re-teaching is commonly required (assuming adequate feedback has been received) but you need to allow enough time for it. Often teachers attempt to "cover" so much material in a short period that a superficial job is done and no time can be spared for remedial or corrective instruction.

Clarity Idea XIX. Use supplementary audio-visual materials to increase clarity and comprehension. It is easy and convenient to use words only in

teaching and we all succumb to the temptation. We must remember that the

spoken word is the most abstract of commonly used methods to communicate ideas.

It employs only the sense of hearing and but one entry into a person's conscious-

ness. In general the eyes are better learners than the ears and perhaps the

ratio is even as high as, "one picture is worth a thousand words." Many ideas

cannot be expressed in pictures and I am not advocating picture books for

instruction. As a supplement to the spoken word, however, they are invaluable.

This calls to mind a general principle very useful in teaching. The closer

to reality are your instructional techniques the more effective your efforts

will become.

An example of this concept can be shown in this situation. If you wanted

to teach about Chartres Cathedral the following steps show how the various

levels decrease the abstractness and increase the concreteness of the learning.

Level I - Tell about Chartres Cathedral

Level II - Show a drawing of Chartres Cathedral

Level III - Show colored pictures of Chartres Cathedral

Level IV - Hear the organ of Chartres Cathedral

Level V - Show motion-sound pictures of Chartres Cathedral

Level VI - Take a guided tour of the Cathedral and attend a service with the great organ playing.

There are many occasions in which only words, spoken and written can be used to teach. The point I want to make is the audio-visual supplements or even replacements for words will add immensely to the comprehension and retention of ideas.

The following model will show the continuum from the most concrete of learning situations to the most abstract.

Proceeding from Stage I on the abstract side where only one sense, hearing, is involved in developing comprehension, we move to Stage II where the sense of sight is used. Stage III adds reality by visualizing concepts through drawings and idea models. Actual pictures and sounds of the objects being studied provide even more accurate representation in Stage IV. In the next stage, V, sound, pictures and motion give a realism not so far encountered. Stage VI adds to the preceeding step the sense of immediacy found in knowing that the event being watched is taking place as you watch. Stage VII makes use of small reproductions in three dimensions of the material under study. Stage VIII engages other senses such as kenesthetic and olfactory and shows actual specimens of things involved in learning. In Stage IX the student comes into contact with the issue or problem and is transformed from an observer to an active

TEACHING MEDIA CONTINUUM
(Abstract to Concrete)

Most Concrete Methods

Stage I	Stage II	Stage III	Stage IV	Stage V	Stage VI	Stage VII	Stage VIII	Stage IX	Stage X
Spoken Words	Written Words	Drawn Representation of Ideas: Maps Charts Graphs Etc.	Still Pictures Records Audio Tapes Etc.	T.V. Tapes Films Etc.	Live T.V.	Exhibits Models Mock-ups Etc.	Seeing and Handling Actual Objects	Arti-ficial Made-up Learning Situations	Real Life Learning Situations

Most Abstract Methods

participant albeit in an artificial situation (i.e., a mock trial). Finally Stage X puts the learner into the middle of a real-life experience where he/she is not an actor but uses all the senses and feels the immediacy and realism of the situation.

The variety of options available to you as a teacher is abundantly clear. A fundamental ingredient of sound instruction is clarity. One of the most effective ways to achieve it is to use the most concrete and sense employing teaching techniques you can with good judgement under your own particular circumstances.

An ultimate test of your success as an instructor will be the extent to which you can make the material to be learned clear to your class. It takes a good deal of thinking, of skill practicing and of caring to do it well. In the end it will repay your best efforts.

CHAPTER 8

NO CONTROL? . . . . NO LEARNING!

The dream ideal in teaching would be to have classes of happy, well adjusted students, working on meaningful, relevant tasks, provided by an instructor who is loved and respected by all, in a subject area which everyone adores. This lovely situation will not be found in many real life classrooms, unfortunately. Instead there will often be some persons who are unable to control themselves, for a host of reasons, and therefore have trouble in accommodating themselves to learning in a group setting. Because this is a very real problem we will now concentrate on what can be done to maintain a reasonable learning atmosphere in the classroom.

Discipline within a group of students simply refers to that condition which permits any type of learning activity to operate successfully. It may result from the willingness of the individuals to voluntarily cooperate, or may require externally applied pressure toward this end. Since you are the educational leader of your group it is your responsibility to see that a proper environment is established. In attempting to achieve this you may find it hard to maintain a sound balance between friendliness and firmness. There are no iron-clad rules on this matter because such variation exists among teachers and student groups. You will need to follow the Biblical injunction to, "Work out your own salvation in fear and trembling." By this I do not mean that research and experience cannot offer many worthwhile ideas to help you. This chapter will be devoted to offering you suggestions and pointers which can help you develop your own "class control style". Each of you can adopt or adapt these notions, amalgamating them with your personality and philosophy of teaching. In the end you will build an approach which allows sound learning to take place and with which you will be comfortable.

Let us begin by citing some of the common problems which might face you as you teach student in groups.

Lack of Attention - daydreaming, sleeping, reading outside material.

Talking - when they should be listening or working.

Individual Disruptive Actions - whistling, banging or other noise-making activities.

Small Group Disruptive Actions - between or among a few students.

Defiance of Teacher - refusal of reasonable requests by the teacher.

Verbal Abuse Between or Among Students - varies in intensity depending on the individual personality clashes involved.

Fighting Between Students - occurs seldom but often enough to be aware that it does happen.

Verbal Abuse or Threats to Teacher - also rare but should be of some concern.

Physical Abuse of Teacher - takes place very rarely despite sensationalized publicity.

This list will cover the great majority of the troubles the typical teacher will encounter. Much will not take place at all but it is wise to give some thought to all possibilities and consider potential avenues of prevention and response.

One of the fundamental laws for the long term control of any disciplinary problem is to determine the cause(s) of the activity. Actions arise out of the individual responses to stimuli and if you can find out the underlying reasons for behavior you are in a better position to deal with it. In your efforts to discover these factors I would like to suggest two worthwhile sources of information.

First. Read about the age level student you are teaching in any number of sound books on developmental psychology. These volumes will describe and analyze the stages, patterns and characteristics of various maturity levels. If you realize, for example, that a particular age group often encounters real insecurity problems, or has difficulty in getting along with the opposite sex, certain reactions in class may be explained. When you understand that learners are passing through a stage of development not only is it easier to tolerate their efforts to deal with the pressures they feel, you will be better equipped to handle the situations which are created. A classic work in this field is, Youth, The Years From Ten to Sixteen, by Gesell, Ilg and Ames, and you are strongly urged to read all or parts of it, most appropriate to your situation.

Second. Find out about the individuals in your classes. We know that each person lives his/her life within an environment and in circumstances which differ in some degree from those of others. These variables, combined with diverse personality types, mental abilities and past experiences result in patterns of behavior which are unique to each human being.

How can you discover some of these important facts which will help you understand the actions of your students? If you teach in a regular school, files are usually kept by guidance counsellors with pertinent data on each student. These documents should be examined not to snoop, but as an aid to teaching. The information you find must not be viewed as "positive" or "negative", but as material which will enable you to more clearly see each student as a separate person.

As a supplement to this source I recommend that you keep your own record of personal background for each learner. The particular items to be included can be selected by you for their value in your teaching situation. As an example the following "Personal Data Sheet" may serve as a starting point to be modified as you wish. With this material at your fingertips vague, shapeless shadows will begin to emerge as more clearly defined figures with personal features and individual characteristics.

PERSONAL DATA SHEET

Date:_____

Name:_____

Address:_____ Phone:_____

Age:_____

Father's name and address: Mother's name and address:

_____   _____
_____   _____
_____   _____

        Occupation:_____   Occupation:_____
        Education:_____   Education:_____
Number of children in family:_____   Brothers:_____ Sisters:_____

Hobbies:_____   Extra-curricular Activities:_____
_____   _____
_____   _____
_____   _____

Courses being taken this semester: Standardized Test Scores: (Completed by
                                       teacher if applicable)

_____   _____
_____   _____
_____   _____

Are you employed?_____   Where?_____

     Kind of work:_____

Plans after graduation:_____
_____
_____

Any physical disabilities or diseases?_____

Additional information:_____
_____
_____

After you have learned about the general behavior and maturity patterns of your students plus something of their personal backgrounds, it is wise to consider some of the reasons for misbehavior in a classroom setting. As was mentioned before, attempting to identify causes is of basic importance to sound, long-range solutions to behavior problems. It is not easy to do, however. Human beings are complex and since modern society places many stresses on all of us, reactions are not always easily traceable to causes. This must not discourage us from seeking out the reasons, however. As a beginning point in understanding the dimensions of this matter the following list is offered as suggestive and illustrative but by no means exhaustive.

Some Causes of Behavior Problems

1. Boredom - Students may regard the work in the class as too difficult, too easy or too irrelevant to be worthy of effort.

2. Personality Clashes Between (Among) Students - The social structure of a class may cause trouble if conflicting individuals or cliques are near one another.

3. Personality Clashes Between Student(s) and Teacher - This may develop through no fault on your part. Try as we might there will be some pupils who simply do not like our "personality style".

4. The Teacher's Actions - The way we handle persons or groups may be very irritating to them. Objective self-analysis regarding our patience, courtesy and sensitivity to feelings can pay real dividends in better relationships.

5. Personal Problems of Students - Sometimes the causes of disruptive actions may have little to do with what is going on in class. Troubles with

parents, peers, employers, girl/boy friends, etc., can trigger behavior problems in class.

6. Revolt Against Authority Figure - This reaction is not uncommon among all age levels but is especially noteworthy with immature young people.

7. Desire for Attention - The need to be noticed, for whatever reason, is strong among some individuals and may result in a fracture of sound learning atmosphere.

Your search for the causes of discipline problems may take you beyond the categories mentioned above. Remember that sometimes you will not be able to isolate the reason(s) for behavior troubles even though you try. If you have been objective and open-minded in collecting relevant information and analyzing the problem but still cannot come up with a reasonable answer - do not over-worry about it! If you show yourself to be a decent, fair human being many of these problems will take care of themselves. A teacher has only so much "worry capacity" and time to expend on these matters without endangering good mental health.

Thus far we have been dealing with types and causes of disruptive behavior. The remainder of our consideration will be divided into two parts. First, we will examine ways in which misbehavior problems can be prevented and second, the treatment of such troubles, if and when they arise, will be covered.

Preventive Discipline

The prevention of disciplinary problems is, of course, the most effective approach to the situation. This is easy enough to say but a good deal harder to do. You must remember that there are no fool-proof recipes which will always work. Keep in mind also that to change behavior often takes longer than you might imagine. With these cautions before you let me suggest some ideas you can use to forestall the onset of disruptive class activities.

Prevention Idea I. Know Yourself. If problems arise the wise teacher examines his/her own behavior first; the foolish teacher blames everyone else! Before trouble arises it helps to ask yourself a few questions and to answer them honestly.

How sensitive am I?

What kind of problems threaten me?

What kinds of behavior and personality types repel me?

Do I consider all student misbehavior to be aimed against me personally?

Do I tend to make stereotyped judgments based on looks, race, sex, social class, intelligence, etc.?

How patient am I?

Do I become angry easily?

Prevention Idea II. Consider the Health of Your Students. I am not suggesting that most of your disruptive students are sick! You may be surprised, however, to find out how many of your learners have minor or even major health problems. Any experienced teacher can tell you about instances in which disease has affected behavior. Consult the school nurse for what information she may have. Observe individuals closely for hearing, seeing or other noticable difficulties, not only for the physical inhibition to learning but the psychological effect as well.

Prevention Idea III. Know and Adjust to the Academic Aptitude of Individual Students. You are well aware, in the abstract, that students come in a variety of "academic packages". To come face to face with this reality in the classroom will bring the idea home to you very quickly. Bright students sometimes cause problems out of boredom, but the greater difficulty arises from slow students. They often feel "punished" for being unable to learn at normal speeds and react out of frustration. It would help you to take at least three actions:

A. Adjust the academic burden through differentiated assignments, etc.

B. Set expectation levels for achievement at realistic levels.

C. Create situations in which slower students can achieve success.

Prevention Idea IV. Become Familiar With the Home Environment of Your Students. Most teachers come from middle class homes where education is valued and language standards are high. Cultural shock sometimes sets in when they encounter pupils from homes where cheating, lying and "gutter language" are not condemned. Other situations in a student's home life can affect classroom behavior. For example, over-strict parental discipline may cause them to resent any "authority figure". Also family fights or pending divorce actions may "emotionally bruise" students so they lash out in reaction.

Prevention Idea V. Have Your Lessons Well-Organized. Know what you want to do and do it. This will create the idea that you are prepared and ready for a successful learning period. Careful and systematic planning will enable you to do this.

Prevention Idea VI. Keep Your Lessons Moving. Numerous and/or lengthy pauses where nothing happens or where there is confusion encourages students' attention to stray and disruption begins.

Prevention Idea VII. Do Not Let Little Things "Get Your Goat". Treat minor things as minor and overlook some small matters. Students can be masters at irritating those teachers who become upset by every noise, look, or action not directly related to the lesson. In this regard a good rule to follow is to "underreact" rather than overreact to less serious disciplinary problems.

Prevention Idea VIII. Maintain a Professional Stance in Relation to Your Students. Remember that you assume verbal roles in the classroom. Among these are not only those of "friend", "counsellor", and "teacher", but "leader", "disciplinarian" and "judge of achievement". Each of you must find that "golden mean" of being "fair, firm and friendly" which will create a good learning atmosphere and with which you can be personally comfortable.

Prevention Idea IX. The Best Way to Discipline Problems is to Employ Effective

Teaching Methods. Those classes which are treated with courtesy and sensitivity, in which a variety of learning activities are used, where assignments and expectation levels are differentiated and in which learners work at useful, interesting tasks will not cause many control problems.

Prevention Idea X. Show Enthusiasm and Vitality In Your Teaching. These qualities are catching and can help create a positive mood in your classes. Unless you demonstrate that you enjoy the teaching - learning process don't expect that attitude from your students.

Prevention Idea XI. Insure a Good Quality of Physical Environment in Your Classroom. Make it a rule to see that the room has fresh air, reasonable temperature, adequate light and is relatively clean and uncluttered.

Prevention Idea XII. Begin Class Promptly. This forestalls the opportunity to start trouble in the vacuum formed by late starting lessons. It indicates purpose and organization thus creating a business-like attitude toward the work. Mechanical duties such as taking roll and signing excuses must often be handled before teaching. You can involve your group before doing this paper work. Ask them to do something definite, i.e. "open your books to page_____ and note these ideas", "start thinking about the answer to this question on the board" or "look over this handout as we will be working on it today".

Prevention Idea XIII. Observe the Common Social Courtesies Toward the People in Your Class. Treat them as you would like to be treated. In some classes the relationship between teacher and pupils appears to be that of "master-slave". If you employ kindness, sensitivity and thoughtfulness in dealing with students you are setting a good example and these feelings are often returned to you.

Prevention Idea XIV. Be On the Alert. The teacher who appears blind or deaf

in a class of active, immature young people is in for trouble. Keep your

eyes and ears open!

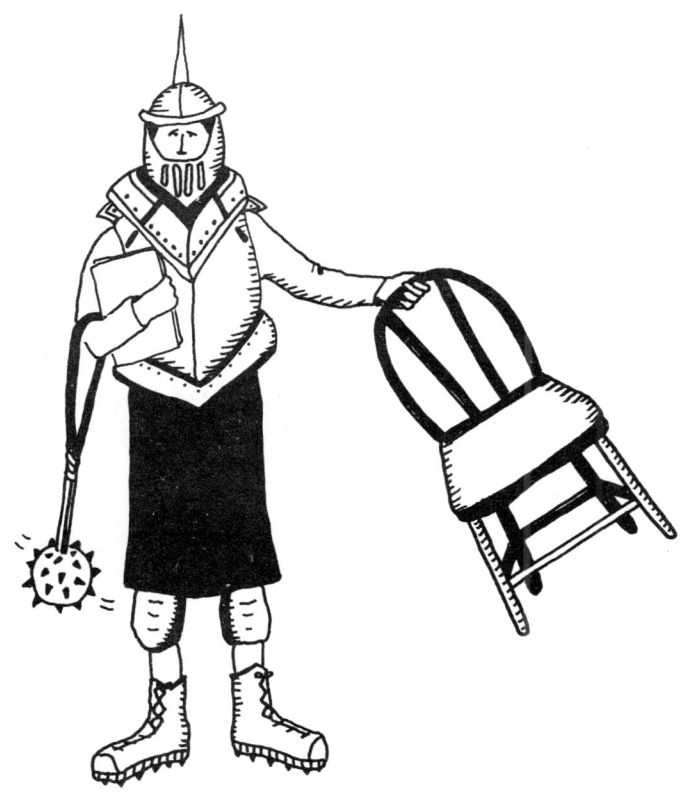

Prevention Idea XV. Do Not Enter a Classroom Expecting Trouble. This attitude

is quickly communicated to students and the "battle will soon be on". An air

of confidence that cooperation will be received from learners will often elicit

that response.

Prevention Idea XVI. Remember That You Will Be "Tried Out". This happens

regularly-especially at the beginning of a term. Pupils are seeking to find

the nature of your disciplinary style and the limits you will allow. When

they discover them the "testing" will drop off.

Prevention Idea XVII. A Few Basic Rules Should be Established and Maintained.

They should be clearly spelled out and violations must be dealt with consistently. Long lists of rules are confusing.

Prevention Idea XVIII. Keep In Mind That There are Certain Times When Disorder is More Likely to Occur. Among these are:

The last period of the day

Ten minutes before lunch

Friday afternoon

Monday morning

Before and after assemblies

All day before important all-school events, i.e. the big dance, game, etc.

All day before a holiday

Prevention Idea XIX. Show Students You Like Them and Want to Help Them. Here talk is cheap - it is your action which will really impress. A few suggestions to help you do this are:

A. Learn student's name quickly and use it.

B. Offer, and follow through, with special help for those having problems with classwork.

C. Chat informally with students before and after class.

D. Know about extra-class activities and outside interests of your students and speak to them about these matters.

E. Attend school functions, such as plays, concerts, athletic contests, etc., in which your students are involved.

F. Others will occur to you if you are in earnest about showing personal interest and help.

Corrective Discipline

The preceding ideas will, if followed, go a long way to help you prevent control problems from arising. Some things will "slip through the cracks" and disruptions will take place. It is then crucial to deal with them in a firm and enlightened manner so as to reduce their impact and, if possible, eliminate their reoccurance. To help you handle these problems after they surface let me offer some ideas for your consideration.

Corrective Action I. Look Over at the Offender-Meet His/Her Eyes if Possible. This eye contact can be very effective depending on the individual teacher. The intensity of the "look" will vary. You may wish to follow the practice of "Evil Eye Fleegle" in "Li'l Abner" and employ the "single", "double" and in extreme cases the "triple whammy" as a curative device.

Corrective Action II. Walk Over to the Trouble Spot and Continue the Lesson from There. No reference to the problem need be made and usually only a short period of time there is required. Your physical proximity often corrects the difficulty.

Corrective Action III. Call the Offender(s) by Name and Request Order or Attention. This is best done in a matter-of-fact voice without showing great anger or irritation.

Corrective Action IV. Ask the Disrupter(s) to See You After Class. Lay the matter before them in a serious but reasonable way-ask for their cooperation and often you will receive it.

Corrective Action V. If the Problem Continues Indicate that the Seating Arrangement May Have to be Changed. Sometimes breaking up a small group or clique will help to restore order. Warn them before you do it, but do not hesitate to take to take action if it is required.

Corrective Action VI. Make few Threats but Always Follow Through on Them When Necessary. Direct action is always more impressive than talk.

Corrective Action VII. Lay the Responsibility for the Disciplinary Action on the Student(s): The reason for it should seldom be your own anger or frustration. It must be pointed out that the disruption is preventing others from learning. The welfare of the total group must come first.

Corrective Action VIII. Be Careful About Sending an Offender Out Into the Hall. This may be an open invitation to some students to leave the school building or get into further mischief outside the room.

Corrective Action IX. Detention After School Can be Effective But May Cause Further Problems. First of all, you must stay to supervise their punishment. Second, many students have legitimate after school activities such as play rehearsal, athletic practice and club meetings. Third, a number of pupils work after school and detention may cause too much of a hardship to be worth the salutory effect which may be achieved. Consult school policy on this matter.

Corrective Action X. Send the Problem - Maker(s) to the School Office. There are a few situations in which the persons involved must be separated and allowed to "cool down". If someone is sent to the office you should always follow through to see that they arrived and have seen the administrator in charge of all-school discipline. Explanations are required and a conference may be needed. This is a serious step and should be viewed as a last resort after other methods of control have failed. It has at least two potential shortcomings. First, it lets the principal know that you cannot handle your own class. Second, the administrator involved may do nothing to support you and the "trip to the office" can become a farce. See "how the land lies" in this respect.

Corrective Action XI. Do Not Over-Punish Out of Anger. Try to "hate the sin and not the sinner". If possible imitate "The Lord High Executioner" in "The Mikado" when he claims that, "My object all-sublime, is to make the punishment fit the crime".

Corrective Action XII. Avoid Punishing the Whole Group for the Misbehavior of a Few. This "shotgun approach" will cause resentment among those not guilty and create more trouble than it corrects.

Corrective Action XIII. Resist "Nagging" at a Class About a Disciplinary Problem. Teachers who use such expressions as "Let's be quiet, class", or "Now, people", over and over will find they become meaningless, nerve-wracking and worst of all, ineffective.

Corrective Action XIV. Remind Yourself About the Effects of Punishment in a School Setting. Punishment certainly constitutes a deterrent to disruptive behavior but it must be used with care. Keep the following points in mind.

A. Loss of group status or self-worth by an individual who is publicly punished can give rise to the desire to get even with the teacher.

B. The most common by-product of severe punishment is fear and anxiety.

C. Frequent punishment in school helps to condition the student for negative reactions toward the school, the teacher and the learning process.

D. Frequent punishment will lower a student's self-concept and in the long run result in feelings of inferiority.

E. Punishment, in general, is more effective when given in private than in public.

F. Praise, in most cases, is more worthwhile in motivating desirable behavior than is punishment.

Corrective Action XV. Do Not Meet a Student's Anger With An Angry Response On Your Own. This is hard to do when emotions run high. If you engage in this reaction, however, it is likely to escalate tensions and further complicate the situation.

Corrective Action XVI. Report to Physical Punishment Should be Avoided. Hitting a student of "roughing him/her up" nearly always causes more problems than it solves. Also you could be sued! Only two occasions could justify physical force. One would be if you, yourself, were attacked and the other could be when a student is assaulted. If you are a small woman, of course seek help from the school office or nearby male teachers. When you feel a potentially explosive situation could erupt into violence, alert this aid beforehand.

In this chapter many ideas have been presented to aid you in achieving a reasonable learning atmosphere in your classroom. Despite their worries most beginning teachers find that control is _not_ as awesome a problem as they feared it would be. Persistence and determination must be your watchwords. Students must be _convinced_ that you mean business in your efforts to maintain order. The most effective approaches are to _teach well_, _treat causes_ and _deal firmly_, _fairly_ and _pleasantly_ with all your students. It will take some time to work out your disciplinary style and for your classes to adjust to it. It is crucial that a workable and confortable learning environment be established since without it even the brightest and most personable of you will fail as

teachers.

CHAPTER 9

HAVE YOUR STUDENTS LEARNED ANYTHING?

Any enterprise which involves processes, products and aims surely requires judgments to be made regarding success. The extent of growth must be compared to expectations and standards. This matter of "quality control" is, most obviously, an important aspect of the teaching-learning encounter. How well you handle this will influence your effectiveness as an instructor. Unless you can determine the nature and magnitude of student achievement you will be operating in the dark, and equally as bad, so will your learners. Adjustments of the instructional process must be made in the light of information you discover about student progress toward goals. Since this is so vital to sound teaching we will now examine some fundamental ideas which will help you understand how to do it well.

A Few Important Concepts

Let us begin by defining several terms often used in dealing with the subject.

Measurement - the process of determining the quantity of anything - in this case the amount and kind of skills, understandings and attitudes amassed during a particular period of study. It is simply the first step in a complete program of assessment. For example, we may measure that a student got 69 points on a test but this is not too meaningful unless it is compared to some standard. In one case the 69 might be 20 points higher than the next best effort in the

group and would be classified as excellent work. In another it might be the
lowest score and thus be considered very poor.

Evaluation - The process of assessing the worth of any measurement thus
giving a judgment as to its <u>quality</u>, is it "good", "average" or "poor". This
is done by comparing the measurement to a criterion, <u>i.e.</u>, what others in the
same group did, what the teacher expects or what the student has done previously.
It will then take on meaning.

Objectivity - The quality of maintaining impersonal judgment in arriving
at a decision - especially here in the matter of school achievement. In
"objective tests", the biases, personal feelings or prejudices of the individual
<u>correcting</u> the examination will have <u>no effect</u> on whether or not an answer is
correct. Among the common types of times found in "objective tests" are short
answer items with only one right response, <u>e.g.</u> "true-false", "multiple choice",

"matching" and "fill in". More about them later.

Subjectivity - The act of injecting personal feelings, biases or prejudices into the process of arriving at conclusions. "Subjective" test items are those in which the worth of the answers may be influenced by the attitudes of the person who is correcting them. The most widely used instance of subjective items are "essay questions". They will be examined shortly.

Reliability - The quality of being consistent. A "reliable test" is one which would obtain similar results if given again under the same circumstances. It is an important property for measurement instruments to have but does not guarantee a good test. It might consistently provide a poor measure of achievement.

Validity - The attribute of truthfulness. The "valid test" honestly measures what it seeks to determine. This is a crucial matter since without it no examination can be trusted to give accurate results. There are several kinds of validity but the most important type for classroom teachers is "curricular validity". This simply means that a good test will truly reflect what has been taught to students. It should be noted that valid examinations are almost always reliable as well.

In arriving at judgments about student achievement you must be sure that what you do is objective, reliable and valid. The remainder of this chapter will be devoted to showing how you can do this.

When making decisions about learner progress toward goals an early step is to identify possible sources of information available to you. No conclusion can be sound if the data upon which it is based is sparce or inaccurate.

Remember in this connection that when you are attempting to obtain evidence on a variety of learning objectives, different methods should be used to secure it. Using written tests only may result in prejudiced or incomplete data. How you collect achievement information will depend on several factors. Among them are, the nature of the material studied, the type of teaching techniques used, the kinds of students in the class and the learning objectives to be gained.

Keep firmly in mind that evaluation procedures must be incorporated in the planning you do for teaching. Thought needs to be given to the times and types of assessment devices you intend to use as the course, unit or daily plans are put together. Otherwise your program of judging achievement will be haphazard and misleading.

How can you set about collecting evidence which will enable you to make accurate decisions on student achievement? The following possibilities are among the many which lie open to you.

1. Written Work (excluding tests)

    Long themes

    Short papers

    Laboratory reports

    Translations (foreign language)

    Workbook exercises

    Book reports

    Poems

    Short Stories

Etcetra

2. Oral Work

   Individual reports

   Group class discussions

   Panels

   Debates

   Simulation games

   Student made audio and/or video tapes

   Oral drills

   Etcetra

3. Special Performance Work

   Student made art pieces

   Athletic skills

   Musical skills

   Speech and acting skills

   Etcetra

4. Miscellaneous Work

   Student made bulletin boards

   Collections of various kinds

   Community centered work

   Construction of projects (models, etc.)

   Etcetra

This list does not include quizzes and formal examinations as we will

deal with them in detail soon. It is intended to be suggestive only and not exhaustive

Organize Your Efforts

Before we go any further one point must be stressed. The teacher often keeps secret how student work will be assessed. He/she knows the program of evaluation and forgets or refuses to share this knowledge with the class. You owe it to them to inform everyone on this matter, not only as a principle of fairness, but to increase the level of performance by those involved. Make sure your students know how, when, and on what criteria their work will be judged. Very few people like to be evaluated but foreknowledge can reduce the trauma often connected with the process.

This can be handled with a minimum of confusion by doing two things, first, announce in adequate time when you plan to give tests and quizzes. If you intend to have regular examinations, weekly, month, or at other set time intervals make this clear at the beginning of the course. Second, the standards of evaluation must also be clarified. Do you plan, for example, to include spelling, punctuation, grammar and organization of answers in marking essay tests? What criteria will you use a short duplicated form in this marking process. It could contain the important features of a good paper, i.e., spelling, grammar, punctuation, clarity, organization, originality, data used, reasoning employed and strength of conclusions drawn. Although it is extra effort and therefore should be used only on major projects this form can explain your thinking about student themes. They can then clearly understand strong and weak points in their work and thus improve the quality of future efforts.

Teacher-made tests frequently provide a good deal of the "evidence" used in making judgments on student achievement. They are _not_ easy to construct well and, I am sorry to say, are often poorly done even by experienced teachers. For these reasons let us now turn to a consideration of how to handle this chore to everyone's best interests. We will divide the subjects into three main sections.

First - Ideas on test construction in general.

Second - Pointers on writing objective items.

Third - Suggestions on framing and correcting essay questions.

Some Principles of Making up Examinations

When you sit down at your desk to write out a formal test keep the following concepts in mind. They may appear to make test building more complicated but once you master them your exams will be more effective.

Test Idea I. Insure that Your Questions Measure Your Objectives. Consult the aims as you make out test items. In this connection remember that **behavioral objectives** will simplify test construction. (See Point II, below)

Test Idea II. Make Sure You Measure What You Taught. This will help assure the quality of curricular validity referred to earlier. A good way to do this is to have an outline of the subject matter nearby and make sure you have items covering important areas.

You can handle both Points I and II by setting up a simple matrix. Across the top of a piece of paper note the primary goals of instruction. Down the left side place the main subject categories. Draw lines so that across from each subject area and below each goal a square will be found. In each square note the questions which will measure the concept and goal. They can be

abbreviated as follows: T-F (True-False) M-C (Multiple Choice) M (Matching)

C (Completion) E (Essay), etc.

Such a "measurement matrix" would look like this:

GOALS	GOAL I	GOAL II	GOAL III	GOAL IV	GOAL V	GOAL VI
SUBJECT MATTER						
CONCEPT I	T-F MC T-F				C T-F	
CONCEPT II	T-F	C	T-F MC			E
CONCEPT III	MC		MC T-F	M	MC	
CONCEPT IV	MC T-F		T-F		C	T-F

If you will take a little time to do this your tests will truly reflect

instructional aims and the curriculum taught.

Test Idea III. Prepare More Items Than You Plan to Use. By making out 10%

more questions than you expect to include, those of doubtful worth can be

eliminated when the rough draft is revised. These poor or ambiguous items can

be weeded out by allowing your test to "age in the desk" for a day. It is

surprising how quickly bad questions will leap out at you upon a second reading.

If you are still in doubt ask another teacher in your subject area to help you

make a decision.

Test Idea IV. Keep a File of Good Test Questions. Any item which is well-constructed and measures a useful goal should be kept. The same ones should not be used time after time, but a reservoir of worthwhile items can serve as a "core" for an exam. Teachers are busy people and help like this is welcome. My suggestion is to begin with a "core" of perhaps 25-30% of the total number of items made up of previously used items. The remainder would be new or modified. Such re-usable questions can be put on 3" x 5" cards and filed either by type of question or subject area involved.

Test Idea V. Include Items of Varying Difficulty Levels. Most achievement tests are combinations of "speed tests" (timed to see how many items of equal difficulty the test-taker can complete) and "power tests" (using questions of increasing difficulty to see how far the test-taker can go). One of the primary functions of an examination is to discriminate among students on the basis of goal attainment. Those who can answer more and/or harder items must be considered to have done better than those who can only correctly respond to fewer and/or easier ones. You thus need questions running from easy to hard so as to differentiate among various student achievement levels.

Test Idea VI. Questions Should be Placed in a Cycle Order of Difficulty. Many people are gripped by high "test anxiety". If they encounter hard items at the start of an exam they can become discouraged and may give up trying. To minimize this reaction the easier questions should be put first. This can be done either of two ways. One type of cycle would be to set up a gradual increase in difficulty level throughout the entire test. A short cycle can also be used including perhaps ten questions, easy to hard, then beginning again easy to hard over again to the end of the test.

<u>Test Idea VII. Watch the "Vocabularly Load" of Test Items.</u> State your questions in the shortest, simplest and most direct wording possible. Do not make them a test of reading, unless that is what you are trying to measure.

<u>Test Idea VIII. Test Directions Must be Crystal Clear to Students.</u> Most test-takers have had some experience with the standard types of questions. Any variation such as "True-False with reasons" should be carefully explained with examples included if necessary. The rule must be that no student should miss an item because he/she does not know the mechanics of answering it.

<u>Test Idea IX. "Scoring Formulas" Can Be Used to Reduce the Effect of Wild Guessing.</u> We all know there is a 50% chance of guessing right on a two-response item and a 25% chance on a four-response question. Through the use of a simple formula it is possible to counteract this percentage. I recommend its use <u>only</u> on true-false items and only then if you have more than twenty of them as it does take a little time to compute. Your students must be told <u>not to guess</u> on questions about which they have no knowledge but to leave them blank. If they do have an idea of the answer but are not sure they should attempt it.

The formula counts one off for an omitted answer but two off for a wrong one. It works as follows:

The Score = The Number Right Minus the Number Wrong

For example, in a 50 item true-false section if the test-taker <u>leaves out</u> 7 and <u>misses</u> 8 his/her score would be figured thus:

Score = <u>35</u>   Minus <u>8</u>

(Number right - found by sub-   (The number incorrect)

tracting the number left out.

(7) **and** the number incorrect

(8) from (50)

Score = <u>28</u> (35, number right, <u>minus</u> 8, number wrong)

Test Idea X. Test Should be Duplicated for Students Except for Short Quizzes.

There are several reasons why each learner should have his/her own duplicated
test.

A. We tend to comprehend the questions more clearly if they are <u>seen</u>
rather than <u>heard</u> only from the teacher dictation.

B. Each student can proceed at his/her own speed in answering questions.
This is hard to do if the teacher reads the test or must erase some items to
put other ones on the blackboard.

C. It is easier to go back and reconsider questions if necessary.

Test Idea XI. Cheating Should be Discouraged.

Dishonesty on exams is a prob-
lem because of the stress put on marks and the importance of tests in determining grades. It is a sensitive matter and no charge should be made unless
you are <u>sure</u> cheating has occurred. A general statement should be made about
cheating and the penalties involved. A few ways to prevent cheating are:

A. Keep your eyes moving over the room during the test.

B. Move about the room to possible problem areas if you think it may be
taking place.

C. Reverse the pages of a test so that each row or neighbor begins with
a different section of the test.

While you cannot ignore cheating don't turn yourself into an "academic
Sherlock Holmes". You must be <u>absolutely fair and objective</u> in discovering

and dealing with it as false charges can be very damaging to individual and group morale.

Test Idea XII. No Choice Should be Allowed in the Questions to be Answered.

This is a rather unpopular idea with some people but it has sound reasons behind it. Whenever you measure anything for purposes of comparison you must use the same instrument. If you attempt to compare student achievement through tests consisting of different questions you are not using the same instrument. It is hard enough to compare results on examinations even when the same items are answered. It is helpful to recall the dictum, "A test is given to measure individual differences not to take care of them".

Test Idea XIV. Tests Should be Corrected and Returned to Students as Quickly as Possible. This rapid feedback will enhance the educational worth of the examination. Tests can be learning devices in at least three ways.

A. The student can learn through individual and class review for the exam.

B. Learning can take place as the test-taker reads the test itself.

C. The review of results provided by teacher-class analysis of questions and answers can add to understanding.

Constructing Test Items

So much for the general instructions on test construction. Let us now turn to particular types of questions you may want to include in your own examinations. We will deal first with the short answer or objective items after which the essay or subjective questions will be considered.

True-False Questions

This often-used item simply asks the test-taker to make a judgment as to whether a statement is true or false. It can measure a good deal if properly made. Superficially it appears simple to frame, but it is more complex than it seems at first look. The following suggestions can help you in learning to handle true-false items with skill and insight.

T-F Pointer I. On the average, two true-false items can be considered per minute by students.

T-F Pointer II. Avoid making broad generalizations into questions. Words like "always" and "never" often tip off students that such statements are likely to be false. The large number of possible exceptions usually give them away.

T-F Pointer III. Trivial statements usually do not measure anything significant. (i.e. "The color of our textbook is green").

T-F Pointer IV. Be careful with using _negative_ statements as questions. The problem here is that students read the items rapidly, disregard the negative word _be sure_ that it is underlined, circled or capitalized so as to call attention to it, (i.e. NOT, (NEVER), NOWHERE).

T-F Pointer V. Use your own phrasing for questions. If you want to test simple memory power, textbook wording is acceptable. But if you want to find out real understanding use not only different words but new examples as well.

T-F Pointer VI. Make sure true and false items have the same average length. Students sometimes discover that false questions are short and general, whereas true statements often require qualifications which make them longer.

T-F Pointer VII. Avoid patterns of responses in answers. It is easy when you make out true-false items to go on a "true jag" or a "false jag" and make up a dozen or so in a row. Some teachers attempt to overcome this by alternating them regularly. This can be figured out by some students and "free" answers are thus given away.

T-F Pointer VIII. Set up your questions so that answers are written in front of the number of the question for quick and easy correcting. For example

_____1. _____. Line them up so a scoring key can be put on the test
  Answer   Question
paper and wrong answers can be noted without delay.

T-F Pointer IX. A clearly identifiable response should be requested, e.g. "T-F" or "True-False" (written out) of "t" (true) "0" (false). I favor the "t" and "0" as they are more likely distinguishable from one another than the others.

Multiple Choice Questions

In this, as you know, a question is asked and the student chooses from several answers provided, the one he/she thinks is correct. In general it is considered more difficult than true-false since there are four or five possible responses rather than just two. It is also harder to make since you must find at least four or five possible answers. In framing your multiple choice questions consider these ideas.

M-C Pointer I. At least four responses should be provided. This will decrease the chance of "guessing right" which students have with only three possible answers. It also will enhance the validity of the item by requiring more discrimination by the testee.

M-C Pointer II. On the average, the typical multiple choice item usually can be considered at the rate of one per minute.

M-C Pointer III. The question part of the multiple choice item must be clear and contained separately from the possible answers. The test-taker should not need to read the answers to ascertain the question.

M-C Pointer IV. The grammar of the question should not give away the answers. Carelessly made items sometimes have such clues as the question stated in the plural and an answer or two in the singular case.

M-C Pointer V. All answers provided should be plausible to the test-taker. If you include one or more ridiculous or obviously incorrect answers the real choice of response may be reduced to two or even one.

M-C Pointer VI. Questions may be made even more difficult by increasing the similarity of the answers.

M-C Pointer VII. Only one correct response should be included. If several

right answers are listed and the student must select the "most correct" one

arguments may result and frustration increased.

M-C Pointer VIII. As in the True-False item, set up the mechanics of answering

so that the letter of the correct response is placed in a space in front of

the number of the question. (_____1.) Also the answers should be lettered

and placed below the question statement as: 1. - Question statement -

A._____
B._____
C._____   possible answers
D._____

In this way confusion can be avoided and the most rapid consideration of each

item made possible.

Matching Questions

This is really a variation of the multiple choice item. Two lists are

drawn up and the test-taker must match each item in the first list with the

one in the second list to which the relationship is closest. The following

suggestions will help you handle matching questions successfully.

M Pointer I. The mechanics of the item should be set up by having the left

hand list, (questions), numbered, with spaces in front of each item in which

to place the letter of the most closely related item in the right hand column.

(answers)   "Question" column   "Answer" column
_____1.   A
_____2.   B
_____3.   C
_____4.   D
_____5.   E

Do not ask student to draw lines connecting the correct responses - it becomes very messy and confusing to both test taker and corrector.

M Pointer II. Include a few more possible "answers" than "questions". If exactly the same numbers are listed in each column students are helped to guess correctly near the end when a few answers remain.

M Pointer III. Do not make your lists of "questions" and "answers" too long. A general rule of thumb would indicate between 10 and 15 "questions" with two or three more items in the "answer" column. Unusually lengthy matching questions often take a long time to complete and can be too complicated. It is wise to break such long questions into two items of shorter length.

M Pointer IV. Try to place both columns on one page to avoid the confusion of flipping back and forth for answers.

M Pointer V. Matching items can be made more difficult by increasing the similarity of "answers" and "questions". A higher lever of discrimination is thus required. For example, if test takers were required to simply match painters (the "questions") with paintings (the"answers") in general this would be one level of difficulty. A harder list would be to make all the painters and paintings Italian. A further increase in difficulty could be produced by listing only Renaissance Italian painters and paintings, and so on.

Completion (or Fill In) Questions

These are statements with important words or phrases left out which are to be written in by the test taker. They are felt to be generally more demanding since the student must think of the answer rather than choosing one from those supplied by the test. Consider these ideas in making your completion questions.

C Pointer I. Supply enough context to allow the student to answer if he/she can. Without this adequate ratio of words given to words omitted the item can become quite meaningless. The following example from an actual test shows you this hazard.

"1._____ came in _____."

What the teacher wanted was:

"1. Norsemen came in 1001 A.D.!"

C Pointer II. Grammar should not give clues to the answer. An illustration of this situation is the blank following the letter "a"_____which would indicate that the word(s) would begin with a consonant. If you find yourself in this position include both "a", ("an").

C Pointer III. If you are seeking answers in particular units be sure to include them following the blank, i.e._____meters, or _____pounds, etc.

C Pointer IV. Word your questions so that only one answer is correct. Even if you are careful about this you may be surprised at some "right answers" you did not expect. For example: "Columbus discovered America in _____." Possible responses could be "a ship", "the Western Hemisphere", "the Fall", "the 15th century", "the Atlantic Ocean", "October", etc.

C Pointer V. Avoid patterns of blanks which might give away the answer. If a question like this was put "Which country leads the world in steel production? _____ _____ __ _____", the configuration of dashes would help those who did not really know the answer. It could not be "Great Britain", "The Soviet Union", Japan", etc., but must be United States of America.

We have now finished dealing with the objective item. Remember that they can be of real value in measuring student achievement. If carefully made they are able to measure not only knowledge but insight and understanding as well. They also provide breadth of sampling over a subject area and can be corrected without bias or prejudice.

There are some things they cannot do, however, and the essay question can fill this gap. The most widely usable examination will contain both types of items for complete and trustworthy measurement in the typical classroom situation.

Essay Questions

The essay question requires the test taker to supply an extended written response in which higher level mental processes are (hopefully) involved. It is as famaliar to the average learner as is the objective items previously mentioned. While essay tests are easier to make up they are more work to correct than short answer exams. The great value of essay items is that, properly handled, they can measure more than the ability to remember information. Since learning is more than the process of accummulating facts, measurement should involve more than simply testing for factual recall. When an essay question is carefully made and well answered it is possible to see the student's thought process. Such processes as organization, application, evaluation, comparison, analysis, generalization, etc. may be tested through essay items. In addition another advantage is that students tend to use better study habits when preparing for essay questions. Also the problem of guessing on answers is reduced greatly.

While the use of some essay questions has solid value in most tests, if they are used exclusively some serious drawbacks are evident.

1. Those students who write very slowly or poorly are unduly penalized.

2. They provide a poor sampling of the subject area unless the test is extremely long.

3. The "halo effect" tends to bias the teacher unduly in favor of students he/she likes and against those he/she dislikes when marking answers.

4. An accurate comparison of the worth of answers is difficult.

5. Time limits required for responding to questions are hard to estimate in advance.

6. Objective marking may be affected by extraneous influences. When doing this, for example, you may be tired, have a headache or are otherwise indisposed. Your mental attitude may be negative because of any of a number of personal problems. Lastly, the marker tends unconsciously to be more lenient toward those papers he/she reads first and harder on the last ones.

It is possible to counteract most of these problems. The following pointers on constructing and marking essay questions will help you make the most out of this worthwhile item.

When writing out essay questions remember these ideas.

E Pointer I. Avoid the type which are really only simple recall items such as listing, etc. They are better turned into several short answer questions.

E Pointer II. Your wording must be crystal clear and explicit so as to prevent misunderstanding thus encouraging the answers which are honest attempts but do not meet the issue raised by the question.

E Pointer III. "Focus" your questions on definite problems rather than creating such broad items that comparison of answer value is nearly impossible. An overly broad question might be "Discuss World War II". More focused this could read, "Compare the military strength of Germany and France at the beginning of World War II".

E Pointer IV. Include more items with shorter answers rather than a very few long ones. Four half page questions instead of one two page or two one page items will give much better sampling of subject matter.

E Pointer V. You will need to decide whether or not to include grammar, spelling, sentence structure, etc. in your evaluation of answers. Some teachers, while wishing to give the majority of weight to substance not form, still count the mechanics of answers. It can be done by giving two marks, the most important to what is written and another much less crucial to writing style. Your decision should be announced to your class before the test is taken to avoid any misunderstandings.

Marking Subjective Items

The correcting of essay questions has been a constant problem for teachers (students as well). These ideas may help you reduce the subjectivity of the process.

1. Make sure you are in a reasonable psychological and physical state when you mark papers. If not, postpone it.

2. Some teachers try to avoid identifying papers with individual students by giving each person a number or having them sign their names at the end of the test. This may help preserve annonimity but often you know your class well enough to be able to identify particular persons even without a name on the test.

3. One school of marking encourages the teacher to read clear through individual test papers and place them in one of five piles (A - B - C - D - F). Later they should be re-read to make sure each has been judged properly.

4. My favorite approach is to make a "model answer" for every question, incorporating all of the points which could be raised in response. Compare each answer to this model and assign points in relation to the degree of perfection achieved.

5. If you have the time, read the papers again to insure against unfair decisions on worth.

In closing this chapter let me raise the problem of comparison standards. When making a final decision on the value of an individual's effort what means of ultimate judgment will you use? Among those possible are:

1. Your own criteria - have students meet what you feel are reasonable

levels of performance.

2. Other students in the class - how does each student compare with the group average - highest to lowest scores?

3. Past performance and/or potential for achievement of individual persons.

This is a hard question for most teachers to answer. You may wish to use multiple standards and possibly combine all three. No matter what you do the solution to the problem will not be perfect.

Now, hopefully, you know a good deal more about measurement and evaluation than you did before you read this chapter. You can see that this whole business requires thought and work. As you proceed to put some of these ideas into practice keep in mind that the process will become easier as you go along. If you move in a systematic and thoughtful way you can establish a pattern of evaluation which will complement and reinforce your good teaching practices. It is worth the effort!

CHAPTER 10

THE TEN COMMANDMENTS OF TEACHING
(With apologies to Moses and the writers of the King James Version of the Bible)

The practice of teaching, as I have tried to indicate throughout the pre-ceeding pages is a very personal enterprise. This does <u>not</u> at all mean there are no principles, valid concepts or skills involved. Each individual must incorporate these ideas into his/her own "teaching style." This application will be accomplished within the <u>mileu</u> of personality, values, background and ability.

This consideration of "Learning to Teach" will close with a statement of ten "Teaching Commandments." In this day of qualification, modification and extreme flexibility I would like to say that these principles are <u>not</u> subject to much revision. They are truths which can stand a good deal of scrutiny and still retain their worth. With that statement and due apologies for oversim-plification of some complex issues let us proceed.

Commandment I. Thou shalt know thy subject. Thou canst not teach what thou knowest not. Thou canst not properly organize, structure, sequence or clearly explain ideas without knowledge.

Commandment II. Thou shalt know thy learners. Thy teaching shall consist of bringing knowledge and learners together and if thou knowest not the nature and background of thy learners what profit shall come from this?

Commandment III. Remember to plan carefully as it is the golden key to successful teaching. Without it there is likely to be weeping, moaning, and gnashing of teeth (mostly the teacher's).

Commandment IV. Thou shalt know the skills of teaching and practice them with insight all the days of thy teaching life. They are the means of translating potential into actuality.

Commandment V. It shall be thy pleasure (and duty) to teach thy learners the skills of acquiring knowledge and wisdom. Remember that without the ability to engage in learning activities such as reading, discussing, thinking, etc., the door to appropriate achievement will remain closed to thy students.

Commandment VI. Thou shalt keep always in thy view the aims to be achieved, for without such clear stars to guide thee thou art likely to wander in the desert.

Commandment VII. Remember that evaluation and feedback are to the teacher what the compass is to the mariner, keeping both on their appointed courses and indicating how close the goal is.

Commandment VIII. Thou shalt organize, structure and sequence what is to be learned in the most understandable and logical manner. In this way thou shalt provide a clear and coherent pathway to the desired prizes of learning and understanding.

Commandment IX. Thou art responsible for creating and maintaining an atmosphere in the classroom in which learning can take place. In this endeavor thou shall remember to be firm, fair, and friendly in all thy dealings with students.

Commandment X. Keep constantly in thy mind that the clear communication of ideas, so essential to learning, cannot take place when word meanings are unknown to learners. Suit thy language to the level of student understanding so that thy teaching will prosper.

Now all that remains is to wish all readers good luck in their journey to become effective instructors. Some of you will take longer to reach your goal than others but do not be discouraged. Good teachers can be made and are not always born.

Keep these Ten Commandments and you will be well on your way to success!

OTHER TITLES AVAILABLE FROM
CENTURY TWENTY ONE PUBLISHING

NEW DIRECTIONS IN ETHNIC STUDIES: MINORITIES IN AMERICA by David
    Claerbaut, Editor   Perfect Bound   LC# 80-69327
    ISBN 0-86548-025-7 $9.95
COLLECTING, CULTURING, AND CARING FOR LIVING MATERIALS: GUIDE FOR
    TEACHER, STUDENT AND HOBBYIST by William E. Claflin   Perfect
    Bound   LC# 80-69329   ISBN 0-86548-026-5 $8.50
TEACHING ABOUT THE OTHER AMERICANS: MINORITIES IN UNITED STATES
    HISTORY by Ann Curry   Perfect Bound   LC# 80-69120
    ISBN 0-86548-028-1 $8.95
MULTICULTURAL TRANSACTIONS: A WORKBOOK FOCUSING ON COMMUNICATION
    BETWEEN GROUPS by James S. DeLo and William A. Green   Perfect
    Bound   LC# 80-69328   ISBN 0-86548-030-3 $11.50
LEARNING TO TEACH by Richard B. Dierenfield   Perfect Bound
    LC# 80-69119   ISBN 0-86548-031-1 $10.95
LEARNING TO THINK--TO LEARN by M. Ann Dirkes   Perfect Bound
    LC# 80-65613   ISBN 0-86548-032-X $11.50
PLAY IN PRESCHOOL MAINSTREAMED AND HANDICAPPED SETTINGS by Anne Cairns
    Federlein   Perfect Bound   LC# 80-65612   ISBN 0-86548-035-4
    $10.50
THE NATURE OF LEADERSHIP FOR HISPANICS AND OTHER MINORITIES by
    Ernest Yutze Flores   Perfect Bound   LC# 80-69239
    ISBN 0-86548-036-2 $10.95
THE MINI-GUIDE TO LEADERSHIP by Ernest Yutze Flores   Perfect Bound
    LC# 80-83627   ISBN 0-86548-037-0 $5.50
THOUGHTS, TROUBLES AND THINGS ABOUT READING FROM THE CRADLE THROUGH
    GRADE THREE by Carolyn T. Gracenin   Perfect Bound
    LC# 80-65611   ISBN 0-86548-038-9 $14.95
BETWEEN TWO CULTURES: THE VIETNAMESE IN AMERICA by Alan B. Henkin and
    Liem Thanh Nguyen   Perfect Bound   LC# 80-69333
    ISBN 0-86548-039-7 $7.95
PERSONALITY CHARACTERISTICS AND DISCIPLINARY ATTITUDES OF CHILD-
    ABUSING MOTHERS by Alan L. Evans   Perfect Bound   LC# 80-69240
    ISBN 0-86548-033-8 $11.95
PARENTAL EXPECTATIONS AND ATTITUDES ABOUT CHILDREARING IN HIGH RISK
    VS. LOW RISK CHILD ABUSING FAMILIES by Gary C. Rosenblatt
    Perfect Bound   LC# 79-93294   ISBN 0-86548-020-6 $10.00
CHILD ABUSE AS VIEWED BY SUBURBAN ELEMENTARY SCHOOL TEACHERS by David
    A. Pelcovitz   Perfect Bound   LC# 79-93295   ISBN 0-86548-019-2
    $10.00
PHYSICAL CHILD ABUSE: AN EXPANDED ANALYSIS by James R. Seaberg
    Perfect Bound   LC# 79-93293   ISBN 0-86548-021-4 $10.00
THE DISPOSITION OF REPORTED CHILD ABUSE by Marc F. Maden   Perfect
    Bound   LC# 79-93296   ISBN 0-86548-016-8 $10.00
EDUCATIONAL AND PSYCHOLOGICAL PROBLEMS OF ABUSED CHILDREN by James
    Christiansen   Perfect Bound   LC# 79-93303   ISBN 0-86548-003-6
    $10.00
DEPENDENCY, FRUSTRATION TOLERANCE, AND IMPULSE CONTROL IN CHILD ABUSERS
    by Don Kertzman   Perfect Bound   LC# 79-93297   ISBN 86548-015-X
    $10.00
SUCCESSFUL STUDENT TEACHING: A HANDBOOK FOR ELEMENTARY AND SECONDARY
    STUDENT TEACHERS by Fillmer Hevener, Jr.   Perfect Bound
    LC# 80-69332   ISBN 0-86548-040-0 $8.95
BLACK COMMUNICATION IN WHITE SOCIETY by Roy Cogdell and Sybil Wilson
    Perfect Bound   LC# 79-93302   ISBN 0-86548-004-4 $13.00

SCHOOL VANDALISM: CAUSE AND CURE by Robert Bruce Williams and Joseph
    L. Venturini   Perfect Bound   LC# 80-69230   ISBN 0-86548-060-5
    $9.50
LEADERS, LEADING, AND LEADERSHIP by Harold W. Boles   Perfect Bound
    LC# 80-65616   ISBN 0-86548-023-0 $14.95
LEGAL OUTLOOK: A MESSAGE TO COLLEGE AND UNIVERSITY PEOPLE by Ulysses
    V. Spiva   Perfect Bound   LC# 80-69232   ISBN 0-86548-057-5
    $9.95
THE NAKED CHILD THE LONG RANGE EFFECTS OF FAMILY AND SOCIAL NUDITY
    by Dennis Craig Smith   Perfect Bound   LC# 80-69234
    ISBN 0-86548-056-7 $7.95
SIGNIFICANT INFLUENCE PEOPLE: A SIP OF DISCIPLINE AND ENCOURAGEMENT
    by Joseph C. Rotter, Johnnie McFadden and Gary D. Kannenberg
    Perfect Bound   LC# 80-69233   ISBN 0-86548-055-9 $8.95
LET'S HAVE FUN WITH ENGLISH by Ruth Rackmill   Perfect Bound
    LC# 80-68407   ISBN 0-86548-061-3 $6.95
CHILDREN'S PERCEPTIONS OF ELDERLY PERSONS by Lillian A. Phenice
    Perfect Bound   LC# 80-65604   ISBN 0-86548-054-0 $10.50
URBAN EDUCATION: AN ANNOTATED BIBLIOGRAPHY by Arnold G. Parks
    Perfect Bound   LC# 80-69234   ISBN 0-86548-053-2 $9.50
DYNAMICS OF CLASSROOM STRUCTURE by Charles J. Nier   Perfect Bound
    LC# 80-69330   ISBN 0-86548-052-4 $11.50
SOCIOLOGY IN BONDAGE: AN INTRODUCTION TO GRADUATE STUDY by Harold A.
    Nelson   Perfect Bound   LC# 80-65605   ISBN 0-86548-051-6 $9.95
BEYOND THE OPEN CLASSROOM: TOWARD INFORMAL EDUCATION by Lorraine L.
    Morgan, Vivien C. Richman and Ann Baldwin Taylor   Perfect Bound
    LC# 80-69235   ISBN 0-86548-050-8 $9.50
INTRODUCTORY SOCIOLOGY: LECTURES, READINGS AND EXERCISES by Gordon D.
    Morgan   Perfect Bound   LC# 80-65606   ISBN 0-86548-049-4
    $10.50
THE STUDENT TEACHER ON THE FIRING LINE by D. Eugene Meyer   Perfect
    Bound   LC# 80-69236   ISBN 0-86548-048-6 $11.95
VALUES ORIENTATION IN SCHOOL by Johnnie McFadden and Joseph C. Rotter
    Perfect Bound   LC# 80-69238   ISBN 0-86548-045-1 $4.50
MOVEMENT THEMES: TOPICS FOR EARLY CHILDHOOD LEARNING THROUGH CREATIVE
    MOVEMENT by Barbara Stewart Jones   Perfect Bound   LC# 80-65608
    ISBN 0-86548-042-7 $8.50
FROM BIRTH TO TWELVE: HOW TO BE A SUCCESSFUL PARENT TO INFANTS AND
    CHILDREN by Gary D. Kannenberg   Perfect Bound   LC# 80-69331
    ISBN 0-86548-043-5 $7.95

73